CHRISTIANITY IN AMERICA

A CRISIS

E. G. HOMRIGHAUSEN

THE ABINGDON PRESS

NEW YORK   CINCINNATI   CHICAGO

HOMRIGHAUSEN
CHRISTIANITY IN AMERICA

Copyright, 1936, by

E. G. HOMRIGHAUSEN

Printed in the United States of America

TO

RUTH

1805

TABLE OF CONTENTS

INTRODUCTION

SINCERE lovers of the Church are disturbed by the state of the churches in our country. Certain trends have developed within them to weaken their clear witness and their inner reality. In many local churches the undignified and chaotic nature of the work indicates a lack of true justification for their existence. It is hard to distinguish these churches as other than mere social or educational institutions. Cheap entertainments, petty programs, overactive organizations are in many cases a waste of time and energy and a travesty upon the honor of the Church. Quiet stability, dignified strength, and genuine respect for the holy things of God have flown, and the minister is often helplessly caught in this whirl of wasteful disintegration, or is himself so lacking in true theological vigilance and intellectual integrity, as to unconsciously further this tendency. There are few churches in our country that can escape this ubiquitous and subtle influence.

I am not unmindful of the fact that the churches are still functioning. They have come through the depression heroically, and have acquitted themselves better than have many financial institutions. I am not saying that all American churches are disintegrating, but I am calling attention to the general influence which in many cases has gone far. Yes, people are still attending the churches, adherents are being won, and vast amounts of money are being

contributed to and through their agencies. Young
men of a high type are recruiting for the ministry.
The churches are rendering a remarkable service
not only along religious lines, but in social recrea-
tional and reclamational work. They have cared for
their unemployed and have provided the will to support vast community charitable enterprises. But
these so-called "successful" aspects of our church
life have come easy to us because we had some means
left, and it may well be that many of these things do
not at all reveal strong inner faith. These "successful" standards, if such they may be called, may
be merely a sop to our smugness and may make us
incapable of seeing the crisis that the churches in our
country must face in the years ahead. For us the
struggle against secularism has only begun.

Insidious and subtle forces are at work which the
Church has not yet faced—indeed, in many cases,
has not even seen in their true perspective. These
forces are not so clearly apparent because they live
a disguised life within the churches. The decision
to be a Christian is not hard as yet, nor is the Church
as wholly on the defensive here as it is in Germany
and Russia. The churches have not yet been thrown
back upon themselves to rethink their very reason
for existence as the Church of Jesus Christ. The
choice is not yet between Christ or anti-Christ, truth
or falsehood. It will be difficult to arouse the
churches to a realization of this issue before it arises
in its acute form, but sooner or later it will come, and
the choice will be neither easy nor academic. In that

day no naturalistic theology will satisfy, no com-
promise will be allowed. Churches will then be
Church or no-Church. In that Day of the Lord it
will have to be either-or, either a Church of Jesus
Christ or another kind of institution that cannot be
called a Church. It might have the form of a
Church but its profession will deny the essence
thereof.

This book is aimed at this problem. It is a personal chronicle of faith by a pastor working in "the
field of the world," watching the modern temper as
it affects the life of the pastor and the average congregation, and is written with the local congregation in mind. Only through the integrity of the
local congregation will health come to the universal
Church, and through it to the community. And
only there can a clear witness be born to the sovereign God at the core of the Church's life. We
need not look for revivals to start among the intellectuals.

I am conscious of a theological flabbiness that is
even now holding our popular Christianity in its
grasp, and no help is forthcoming from our centers
of intellectual leadership. They are speculating
doubtingly at the threshhold of a living and positive faith. There is more theological illiteracy
among Christian people than we realize. People
do not know the simple fundamentals of what it
means to be a Christian. They may have their ideas,
but are their ideas supported by responsible and
intelligent leaders? A common conception is that

a Christian is one who "belongs" to the organized
Church. He exposes himself to the "uplifting
ideals" of preachers' "talks." Perhaps he has no bad
habits, or perhaps he conforms to established habits
that are regarded as Christian norms. Christian convictions are not distinctive nor potent. A Christian
is rarely regarded as one who makes a living confession of faith in definite, authoritative facts.

Further, it is my observation that Christian
assumptions which operated in our fathers' lives as
unquestioned and self-evident are held today with
great reservations or as a venerable form—or mostly
not at all. Our general social and political life is
fast losing the assumptions of life that once made
this nation to be regarded as "Christian," in profession if not in absolute practice. Some of these
assumptions were the warp and woof of our American experiment.

The churches at Jerusalem in 1928 regarded
"secularism" as the most dangerous enemy of Christianity. But if this "secularism" of the modern
world has assumed such mighty proportions, and is
still gaining impetus, we might ask ourselves the
humiliating question as to why it was not detected
sooner. Can it be that the very churches of the
West, which undergirded a growing secularism with
religious sanctions, were so blind, and are today so
enmeshed in the secular spirit, that they have lost
their power to discriminate between the voice of the
Shepherd and other voices? Until the Church has
done with "secularism" in its own household, and

hears the voice of the Shepherd only, it should stop criticizing "secularism" outside its walls. No criticism of the enemy will give the critic a positive weapon whereby the enemy can be overcome! How can the Church speak to the world about a sovereign God of all life when it does not worship such a God in its own household? Perhaps a great modern theologian is right when he says that our secularism of the world is, after all, only the shadow of the false sanctity of the Church! By which he means that our world's present religious and social debacle is nothing more than the shadow of the Church's apostasy, its false thinking. The churches have lost their vigorous vigilant and uncompromising obedience to the God and Father of Jesus Christ, and Him alone! To lose this is fatal.

The churches have been making their theologies scientific. That may be well and good up to a certain point. But they have been adopting the world's methods with avidity. They have flirted with modern philosophy and educational theory. They have sanctioned many things that are today turning out to be wolves in sheep's clothing. The adoption of the optimistic idea of man has been a mistake. Had they known their New Testament, they might have known it was unchristian as well! The adoption of the Utopian idea of the kingdom of God as the end of history has also been a travesty. It is proving not only untrue to the faith but a hindrance to a proper influencing of the world with the Christian gospel. It lacks a critical and realistic understanding of man and history, and does not allow an effective method for dealing with social problems.

The wholesale adaptations of modern tendencies have affected the old doctrines such as the atonement, the nature and purpose of Jesus Christ, the idea of the kingdom of God, the Church, and many others. The churches are therefore caught in a confusion of thought that will not be cleared up by more action, but by more mental perspiration and suffering. Churches no longer think sufficiently clearly or sustainedly about the Christian faith to enable them to speak with a strong inner authority born of something beyond mere denominational policy, journalistic claptrap, or pet theologies.

Therefore this book is a symptomatic message coming from one who feels compelled to cry in the wilderness to warn the churches of the impending crisis. I have no illusions as to my success. I care not for success. I have no other desire than to dig deep into the real reason for the existence of Christianity. On the basis of its history, the sources, and the crisis of the hour, I want to know the power of that Reality which is at the heart of the strange and potent movement with which I am connected and of which I am a minister. I am concerned not about academic questions but about the local application and power of that gospel in the life of the churches. The Church is the point at which this Christian power becomes actual in the world in which I live. I am therefore greatly interested in reviving theology, which is not a dead study, but a living and critical re-examination of the inner truths of Christianity. And I am anxious to enlist comrades in this stupendous task, which is the necessity laid upon us in this hour.

I am not a fundamentalist. I realize that there are abiding truths in that camp. But we have outgrown it. We cannot accept its literalism, its alliance with antiquated science. It is too static. It seeks to define too much, forgetting that human definitions are only relative and tentative. It makes God too fixed a Being. It inclines to arrogance and pride. It also tends to dry scholasticism. It is the ghost of the past trying to live in another day.

Nor can I accept the liberal, or modernistic, point of view. It has its merits, to be sure. We owe the liberal spirit much. But liberalism also is a ghost trying to live in a new day. It is too fluid. Its adherents, who a few years back boasted of their broad-mindedness, are today as dogmatic and narrow as the fundamentalists they then assailed. Liberalism is friendly to science, but it gives up the whole Christian case by becoming enslaved to scientific method. It is too intellectual, and inclines to snobbishness. It liberates, but at too great a cost. Its optimism is sentimental. Its condescension to culture is its weakness. It treats sin too lightly. There is not much left of historical Christianity after liberalism gets through with it. It thereby practically liquidates the faith of the fathers and ignores the whole Christian tradition by explaining everything away. It makes of Christianity something new—something that it *was not!* It holds to illusory ideas about a Utopian Kingdom, and dilutes that Kingdom to hardly more than a highly "religious" culture-pattern. It flounders, it has no word for our times, in spite of its busy intellectual activity. It never finds anything, although it has been clearing up the fields a long time. It inclines to an activism that loses the patience of hope, and, like the fundamentalist, takes almost everything out of God's hands by assuming an attitude of proud, self-sufficient human surety. It lacks solid theological ideas. It too finds it hard to give way to a newer type of Christianity. But it must.

I am convinced that the next step for the churches is not an attempt to "whoop up" church life by artificial programs or "drives" for members and money. That is only an alibi for an uneasy conscience. The next step is not the recovery of denominational theologies. Nor is it in an old-fashioned debate between the merits of liberalism and fundamentalism. It is not in a frantic social activity for the sake of bettering the world. All these things may have merit, but only relative and subordinate merit.

Rather, we will need to recover *the* Christian theology, to attain to a strong inner structure of the Church's objective faith from which in the midst of a world that is fast and impatiently creating its own theologies in the vacuum of modern life the custodians of the Christian absolute have unconsciously departed. The churches will need to cease doing everything good that comes along, and give witness and expression to the Only Good at the heart of the Church, that Good which matters more than everything else in all the world.

That Good will not be recovered by proposing some "process" in nature, or some good in mankind as a substitute for the real God. Nor can it be recovered by rehashing old theologies. That Good must be given the simple, strong term "God," and filled with the content that God Himself gave it in the revelation He has given of Himself in the Testaments and in historic Christianity. When that God is again given an opportunity to make Himself known and felt, evangelical churches will possess a stable element at the center that can readily be harmonized with a scientific temper. And we will see a new type of Church emerge, which will be both Catholic *and* Protestant.

We cannot become prescientific obscurantists, nor can we become scientific experimenters. One solution is unrealistic, the other unchristian. But we can be true scientists and Christians too. True liberalism is not incompatible with catholic Christianity, unless such liberalism trespasses its bounds and invades the sacred precincts of that which sinful man can never know, but which God must reveal.

The first part of this book is analytical. It deals with our American church scene in its deeper aspects. I hope these sections may not seem academic, but practical. They have issued out of anguish. This book has been difficult to write.

The second part of the book is designed to be constructive. It is not complete. I invite others to work with me at recovering *the Christian Truth,* which is beyond our creation, or party control, but which is promised to us for our knowledge if we seek it together. If some statements in this volume seem harsh and curt, I assure the reader they grow out of jealous love. I love the Church. I am an American churchman. And I have first criticized myself. My greatest critic has always been the One on the cross, whose judgment has for me condemned as false every basis of Christianity save His sovereign love for the Church. Nothing but this jealous and only love could have initiated the basic facts of the faith by which I as a Christian live. I feel in my soul that the apostasy of myself and my comrades as churchmen, as ministers, has been an apostasy to that love the like of which is not found anywhere else in all the world, and which I, as one of its beneficiaries and ministers, must know with wholeness of soul as I know nothing else.

E. G. HOMRIGHAUSEN.

PART I

CHAPTER I

THE CRISIS

A SHORT time ago there appeared in one of the leading theological magazines of the European continent a very interesting and illuminating article upon the general subject of American theology, written by a Swiss pastor who within the last few years had been an exchange student at a theological seminary in Chicago. Of course it was only an observation, and was not intended to be a comprehensive theological discussion, but it was brought to my attention by a good Swiss friend who thought that American theologians ought to correct some of the impressions which it had created in Europe about the condition of Christianity in American churches.

The gist of the article was that American theology was largely influenced by the "Chicago type" of theology. It stated that American theology is quite generally pretty thin, inclined to humanism and Socialism, that the gospel is largely identified with naturalism, and is a loose program of social betterment, a technique for spiritual development, a human "value" of the highest kind. Christianity here, it held, unlike that in Europe, begins usually with the human being's needs and then works out to God's satisfaction for those needs. This makes for humanism and religious pragmatism. In Europe,

theology begins with God, and from that basis man
is asked to adjust himself to that God, who is forever beyond man's proof and beyond any man's
claim upon Him. Europeans are afraid of our formless and untheological Christianity, as we are of their
formal and theological Christianity. Yet both need
each other.

My conclusions regarding American theology,
while not absolutely in harmony with those of the
article mentioned, would be similar.[1] It is utterly
erroneous to say that all theology in American
churches is dominated only by a psychological and
sociological interest, highly tinged with humanistic
naturalism. If only it were! We might then have
a true barometer by which to judge our atmosphere.

Nor is it possible to speak of an "American theology." We have theologies, but no theology. We
have an American temper that affects all our
churches, even the Roman Catholic, the Orthodox
Lutheran, the Protestant Episcopal, and other strong,
churchly theological types. But we do not have an
American Church. There are many things which
inhere in all the churches because of our peculiar
frontier atmosphere and our air of freedom.

Liberalism is to be found in some manner in all
churches, except perhaps in those strictly disciplined.
But liberalism is only a method and a temper. So
is fundamentalism, whether the general interde-
nominational kind like that of the late William

---

[1] Compare *Union Seminary Review*, Richmond. July, 1935.

Jennings Bryan, or the type that makes fundamentalism a desire to return to the original tenets of any denomination's origin. And fundamentalism is only a method and a temper. But the Christianity of our popular church life in America is neither fundamentalist nor liberal. It is largely a nebulous concoction. It lacks definiteness and depth. It is not clear-cut in its axioms nor does it possess a strong structure of faith in the given facts at the basis of the Christian movement. It ranges from the strict Calvinism of the Christian Reformed group to the nearly "Everythingness" of the Unitarians. Generally speaking, it is a mild evangelicalism, a blend of popular Lutheranism-Methodism-Baptistism - Presbyterianism-Congregationalism, etc. It is a moral idealism tinged with Christian sentiment and phrases. It may mean anything. It is not deeply rooted. It is intensely individualistic; it fears formal and centralized authority; it is aesthetically barren in worship and architecture; it is emotionally and theocratically inclined and represents a formless group of individualistic churches that hardly know the unity of a corporate church life. It is a Christianity that has had but one world-recognized theologian—Jonathan Edwards. Since then, our theology has been in a state of solution.[2] If evangelical Christianity depends

---

[2] Compare the chapter headings in Rowe, *History of Religion in the United States,* The Macmillan Company, 1924, and note how Christianity has been liberalized, rationalized, socialized, spiritualized, psychologized, denominationalized, Americanized so that the *human effects* of Christianity have gained increasing predominance at the expense of the *theological content.* The process of theological solution has worked toward dissolution.

for its existence upon a theologically intelligent constituency in America, I hesitate to predict the future! This, I believe, is the matter with our theology and our churches. Our future will reveal this weakness. It is a weakness of central structure.

The article in question aroused me to think seriously about our American church life in this present crisis. We have many churches. We deplore their number. But that is due to the air of freedom we possess. The restraints of Europe do not operate here. Our churches are free. As a result there was nothing to hinder the rise of our many churches, each claiming (perhaps legitimately) to have discovered some neglected phase of the gospel, which was regarded as most important. I say "legitimately" because all denominations are founded upon some legitimate idea resident in the deposit of Christian faith, whether of healing (Christian Science), the possession of the Holy Spirit (Pentecostals), or of congregational democracy (Congregationalists), etc. The Roman Catholic Church is first of all a *unity* with many household diversities, but popular American Protestantism, by its very lack of unity in the church ideal, became diversified, and is now seeking what unity it can get without giving up its diversity. It is not the number of our churches that disturbs me. The weakness and crisis of modern Protestant churches in America is their lack of the idea of the Church universal. And that lack is due to a lack of theological authority in matters of the faith. We enhance denominational colors, but not *the* sunlight! And that goal cannot be achieved by our church life as presently constituted.

This brings with it our crisis, not only in the American churches, but in American society as well. If our social life lacks the unifying ideal of "Americanism" (an undefined thing which many regard as individual opportunism without the responsibility of a corresponding loyalty), our church life in America lacks the unifying ideal of the Church universal. All through our history we have repudiated the aristocratic form of society. We are rebelliously done with kings and titles of nobility. We started with the freedom of the romantic age, without the background of cultural aristocracy. Today we are struggling to possess some unity that shall redeem our diversity. Individualism and provincialism need the balance of a high unitive authority that is beyond us. This we lack, both in American cultural life and in church life. To many of us it is enervating, and dangerous in the light of the coming issues which the Christian faith must meet as a unit.

To see this crisis in church life is to begin to ask about the ideal of the "holy catholic Church" and how it may be recovered. The "holy catholic Church" means that the Church is a divine idea and creation. At its base there is a *given* foundation. The universal Church exists—whether there are men in it or not! In our American democratic life we have thought of the Church as existing only where there is a company of *men* who voluntarily come together to form a church. We Americans, in our pragmatic way of thinking, have difficulty in conceiving of anything as *existing* apart from that which is tangible. Ideas with us have played small rôles. Our minds are concerned with tangible things, and as such we have lost sight of great realities that exist *a priori*, by and in themselves.

We are activists. Therefore, with us, the Church has no peculiar substance in reality. Our activism is a result of our anti-European tradition, our progressive pioneering, our freedom from the restraints of an aristocratic culture, our inveterate democratic idealism. Churches like the Protestant Episcopal, the Roman Catholic, and other authoritative ones, have had a difficult time in our midst, primarily because they smack of the Old World with its emphasis upon corporate, centralized authority, and formal, aesthetic services of worship. (That is hardly true now, since Americans in their disillusionment concerning their individualism today long for more authority and dignity in church life, and many of the denominations are gradually taking on, in architecture and practice, the form of churchly types.)

But how shall the popular American churches regain the catholic ideal? It can hardly be done through more undirected enthusiasm, more intense provincial denominationalism, more reactionary fundamentalism or nebulous and humanistic modernism.

We need to bridge the gap between the modern American churches and the historic and traditional

Christian Church. Our suspended church life in America has suffered isolation from the whole Christian tradition. Therefore we lack historical perspective and balance. We do not see the Church as a persistent entity with a long and venerable tradition. Our sectarian idea of the Church as separatistic voluntary groups will need to be corrected by a conception of the Church as universal, traditional, and historical. Christianity did not begin with American sectarian church life! It began long ago and has lived in varying expressions all over the world. All this is Church. There is something far more important in the Church than its human varieties. But we have enhanced the human varieties.

We will need to allow the pioneering activist genius to rest for a time, to think more deeply about the foundations of the Christian faith. We can afford to build slower and more surely. Nothing short of developing true theological thinking is involved. The universal Church's strength among us will depend upon the resurgence of *churchly* thinking, which is uncompromisingly based upon the premise of Christian revelation and traditional thought concerning it. Denominational thinking is our curse, and our insufficiency. It is too provincial. It lacks wholeness.

If the crisis of our social life is in the realm of discovering a modern equivalent for a community-ism, or "Americanism," the crisis in our church life is in finding the modern equivalent for the "holy catholic Church." "Americanism" can no longer mean human opportunism without responsible social loyalty to something beyond the individual. It cannot longer mean individual pioneering without mutual responsibility to the community. So Christianity in America can no longer mean religious freedom for the human individual without responsible loyalty to something beyond him which creates the church community. To be a Christian is to be free, but to be free in bondage to the whole Body of Christ's truth!—and its Head! The desire for denominational expression must now be tempered with an intense desire not merely out of expediency to federalize the churches in "life and work," but to bring to bear the absolute unitive demand of the Christian Church and living theology in matters of living faith and conviction.

A mere expedient unity is no unity at all. It is as strong as the weakest link. It is merely a makeshift in which denominations have not given up one whit of their autonomy in the face of the only Christian autonomy, which is the gospel of Jesus Christ. (And that gospel is not a man's religious philosophy!) Denominations still think of themselves as the whole Church. They think first of themselves in secret and denominational council. Our present union agencies are afraid of this essential aspect of unity. But it must be forthcoming if *the* Church of Jesus Christ is going to make a united witness to the truth of the living God to this generation; otherwise in denominational pride the churches will be apostate to this cry of the hour. We do not want a

Christian unity for the Church's sake, but for God's, the gospel's, and man's sake.

There are many implications involved in this idea, all of which are related directly to our popular Christianity living in the American temper. We lack the tragic sense in our history; as yet, no conqueror has ever set foot on our soil. This, together with our remarkable conquest of nature, our reckless progress and our idea of the omnipotence of education, has made us oblivious of the dark depths of life. As a result, we do not have a theology, or a philosophy of life, based squarely and only upon God's gift of Jesus Christ, who is not man's idea, but who is generated by the grace of God. Even the churches have absorbed this temper, with the result that the deeper issues of sin and death and grace and immortality are not sufficiently touched upon. In our emphasis upon the gospel as a practical way to the abundant *human* life we have exalted those things that divide men socially, racially, nationally, and not those that unite us out of the depths of human sin. The popular Protestant churches have not apostatized, so much as they have neglected to proclaim a full gospel. The objective elements in the gospel, which are beyond man's power to create, have been gradually sublimated to those which are subjectively felt. It is no wonder that America became the land of the psychology of religion. It is also the most *active* Christian section in Christendom. The human side of the faith has been emphasized at the expense of the divine.

The churches were, likewise, caught in the great desire for change. Our programs became experiments, in which the constant factors of the faith were forced into such molds that the people within the churches did not know what was objective and what was subjective. This is how we came to regard a Christian as a moral, or "religious," person. Our conformity to the American temper has robbed us of our deeper *Christian* foundations.

This gay spirit of adventure has made us impatient with the realist, and vehement against the pessimist. Our energy has judged anything suggestive of the cross as something quite alien to the facts of life. The idea of the grace of God as the compensation from God, given to us because of our constant failure to fulfill our duties to God, is not a popular doctrine among us. (We are loath to admit our need of grace.) Nor is the reality of sin as a basic factor in the Christian scheme of redemption popular. This world has so many attractions and so many rewards that we have a way of smoothing over all unpleasantries. This is our nature. We do not know the gospel as something that comes to us when we could not create it, nor even control it. We do not know it as God's gospel!

We have never had a state, or people's, Church. Our churches have always been voluntary associations. As such they are provincial, not broadly human or *theo*-logical. State churches always conceive of Christianity as a broad social necessity which vouchsafes to all a minimum religion, and includes all men in its bosom as gospel-directed human beings. With us, religion has never had such a meaning. Our churches lack comprehension. While our nation does profess a popular type of Christian faith, since the President takes an oath upon the Bible, and the legislatures open with prayer, etc., nevertheless, State and Church are separate. Roger Williams is the typical American in this respect. Therefore religion is not taught in the public schools, and people are free to be free of any and all religion! This has made for bad effects. One is that our churches are exclusive. Another is that many children grow up religiously illiterate, and we are thus unable to maintain the tradition of keeping the United States a Christian nation on the ground that the majority of its citizens are Christian. Still another is that the churches are being supported by people who do not have a religious training that is proportionate to their training in the public schools. As a consequence, the churches suffer through theological anaemia.

Still another is that the churches have perpetuated our social divisions. Coupled with these conditions, we find the clergy less able to think systematically because of the popular mood and the rush of clergy life, with the resultant effect that the Church no longer can claim a strong existence, because of inner weakness, enervating diversity, and lack of an intelligent ministry whose business it is not merely to administer churches, but to be expert in the Church's divine science of life. All this aggravates our crisis.

But our freedom from the State can be our greater advantage—*if* the churches arouse themselves into a healthy inner strength in time! Theological intelligence alone based upon God's truth can redeem our Protestantism, just as political intelligence based upon the facts of human existence alone can redeem our democracy.

Our sectarian idea of the Church, with its extreme democracy, also aggravates this crisis. When laymen control the church, one usually finds them to be Christians of a high type. But when the ministry is not highly regarded; when the minister is not trained (perhaps fifty per cent of our clergy are not college or seminary trained) or alert; when he is forced by the nature of the modern active church to abandon his study, or is dictated to by those who control his salary, the Church is not free to exercise its franchise of freedom in the gospel. The Church then loses its vigilance because it lacks the strength of *deep* knowledge and mature breadth of experience. It is controlled by untrained men and common custom and not by its true Lord who gave it birth. Most of our church laymen are not capable of making theological distinctions. They have no time for it, nor can they practice the vigilance needed to keep the gospel pure. Where the ministry suffers for lack of theological experience, the message will soon be diluted with many things not true to the faith.

Again, we in the American churches criticize the European churches for their close relation to the State. But we are just as attached to the current ideas of "democracy" and "liberty." Democracy and liberty can be immoral too. We also are enslaved! Churches may be secularized by too close relations with the social environment. The advantage might lie as much on the European side of historical experience and tradition as on the side of our unhistorical adolescence and untrammeled freedom. The one needs the other. But, for us, living in this land, the signs of the times point to the necessity of a redemption of our shallow and diversified church life by the emergence of a real concern for a deeper theology grounded in the given and unitive Christian revelation. Good as may be the American ideas of democracy and freedom, and good as may be the European ideas of corporate and aristocratic life, *these* are not the entities which give life and existence to the Church. The Church lives by a higher necessity than anything human, however noble, even though it may find it good to bless, to a limited extent, certain social ideas. The true Church must not be bound by social ideas and political ends. And to escape such slavery, the Church must critically know its own reason for being.

The churches in America, however, are too much bound to human interpretations of the gospel, which have been torn out of the context of the *total* Christian doctrinal fabric. No denomination can honestly say that it contains all the Christian truth, and none could dare proselyte with the egotistical idea that to win others to their denominational confession would be to win them to the true Church! Most of our denominations are either bound to old national types, to the cultural ideals of the United States, to racial diversities, to class types, or to some other emotional or ethical peculiarity, which could be traced down to a human effect of the objective gospel. As long as there is no honest confession born of a broader vision in the households of these camps, it is hard to envision a united Church, united not for love of *physical prestige* or *earthly pomp*, but united for the sake of giving the Gospel of Jesus Christ a pure, positive, and strong witness to the world. No unity that is based on anything less than God's sake is worthy the name, nor will it confront the world with the God and Father of Jesus Christ for whom the world waits, whether the world articulately knows it or not. It is not the churches, or the Church, of *man* that counts in the end. It is the truth of the living God. And only in witnessing to it can the Church be saved. Only in obedience to the truth can a Church be Church.

It may be claimed that we are moving toward such a unity today. Yes, and no. True, we have many united agencies, from religious education to missions and to world peace. A real working nucleus of ecumenical spirit is at work in all the non-Roman Catholic Churches of the world. The laymen have union organizations. Theological training is becoming less denominational. Books have broken down the denominational walls. Many denominational leaders rise above their camps. There are many other factors that indicate a growing unity. But these are not enough. We need something positive, something more than expedient.

The confessions, or denominations, are, after all, our official channels of Christianity. Even the community churches seem to be becoming a denomination. There are indications that denominational walls are being strengthened in the face of many influences that work for their demolition. Our federal agencies are still secondary to denominational interests. Soon or late, our federal union agencies will meet a crisis. In that day it will be revealed whether or not these union forces have the essential "stuff" in them, born of obedience to the gospel of God, that will provide them with enough organic life to withstand the traditional nature of the denominations. Union efforts will then either fall of their own weight or they will stand of their own strength. It must not be forgotten that denominationalism is still strong and the official channel of Christianity in America. Union efforts derive their authority from whatever the denominations desire to give them, which concession is not enough to affect the strength of the denominational groups. Present union movements are based upon too sentimental and shallow a basis. They lack churchly integrity and strength. Good as these efforts are, and necessary, they will need more than popular sentiment to support them in the day that is ahead. Federalism must be careful not to become another type of denomination. It must attract a group of thinking persons to undergird it, not with more than expedient denominational polity, but with the vital force of the Church's essential *faith* and *witness*.

There are other forces at work in American church life which have a bearing upon our crisis. We have experienced the breakdown of our optimism. Unemployment, the rise of the class struggle, the depression, the checking of our energetic prosperity, the defeat of Prohibition, the disillusionment following the Great War as regards a warless world and a world of democracy, our criminal record, our political "gangsterism," and many other hard facts have shocked us into seeing life in other than optimistic terms. There has been an increase of suicides. The unrest over government experiments, and the talk of embarking on a new era bring uncertainties that are anything but comforting to optimists. We have been driven to see a little of the tragic side of life. The confusion of the press and the radio, and even of the pulpit, has turned the thought of many Americans inward. Life is no longer so simple. While there is no conclusive evidence that this has worked for a revival of church life, it has its effect nevertheless upon our mentality. Our progress has been stopped. We are coming to be done with our own authority. There is abroad a deep desire for superhuman authority. (The ground is ripe for dictatorial absolutes. Let us hope the True Absolute is enthroned.)

This is foreboding, at least for churchmen. It has made them stop and consider the relation of the church's life to the social debacle. They have asked themselves honest questions about the power of their gospel to deal with disillusioned people, with the gigantic forces of the social order. In fact, the depression and its aftermath in the lost morale of many church people, is a crisis for the current, popular message of the churches. It is a Day of Judgment for much that passes for church work, worship, service, preaching, teaching. Churchmen are beginning to see that in such desperate straits, the gospel must have one message, which must reach men. And the gospel cannot be man's wisdom. It cannot be less than a gospel from the only living God. There is a sign of the times in this situation, which, if men read aright, has much to say to the American churches about their common gospel.

True, among the popular churches in America there is a common attitude toward doctrine, forms of worship and expressions of Christian conduct. Members of various churches transfer from one to the other, scarcely noting any difference. The radio, highways, press and school have welded us together into a more homogeneous culture. We speak one language—American, not English. Sheer community of business life has produced a social unity that the churches cannot but feel. Yet it is impossible to conceive of a *real* Christian Church emerging in America on a *social* basis, not only because it is socially impossible but because such a unity would not be a witness to that which is at the heart of the Christian faith. Any unity that issues as a mere community expedient is not a real Christian, or divine, unity. It may become such in time, but it lacks organic strength. It does not witness to God's truth, which is the important thing. (And only in God is there true human unity.) Churches of such a union may do effective work together, but they lack the fundamental nature of a true Church. For this reason it is impossible as well as undesirable to conceive of a national Church of America based entirely upon social grounds. Such a Church might be efficient, but it would betray *the* Church's task. Yet we are witnessing a homogeneous trend in our country, not so much along cultural lines as along what one should call economic and temperamental lines. It has its effect upon the churches. Let us hope it will not force the churches into a false unity merely for the sake of supplying spiritual sanctions for this undefined "Americanism," or the community in which the churches are located. Only one other development can forestall such a forced unity—that is a unity based upon the only unity the Church of Jesus Christ can have, a unity in its central nature and function for the truth's sake. Before that can come American churches may need to suffer. Out of that suffering there will come a creative desire and necessity to rethink seriously, in terms of modern life, the meaning and authority of the gospel for our day. That thinking will be obediently true to God's voice and will. It will be a type of thought that centers in Christ.

Only such a desire to rehabilitate the reason for the existence of a Christian Church will help to make the churches strong by becoming professing bodies, and confessing to faith in the living God who was in Christ.[3]

The American churches will need to grow up, to cease this undirected and feverish activism and shallow sentimentalism. They will need to recover the idea of the "holy catholic *Church*" with all its implications. They will need to see *the* faith in the light of nineteen hundred years of Christian history. They will need to repent of their rebellious isolation from the whole body of Christ. They will need to recover a firmer foundation than that which is now undergirding our churches. They will need to make unity not so much a matter of expedient federalism that still allows the control to stay in the hands of the denominational groups that hold the ultimate power, but instead, they must create a real body of living theology which will stand in its own right. They will need to detach themselves from democracy and freedom, even though they must live in their atmosphere, that they may not be slavishly involved in the coming struggle, when these terms will be used by groups that have no concern for the Christian ideal of democracy and freedom, tempered by the authority of the gospel. They will need quietness. They will need quality. They will need to heed only the voice of the true Shepherd, who alone can instruct the Church of His fold.

[3] Confession means a serious affirmation of the object of faith. As such, living creeds are battle cries, calls to arms, action and struggle. A confession is not a definition so much as it is a living commitment of life to its object of absolute trust. A Christian confession is not individual but group affirmation.

In place of the pioneer must come the statesman. In place of the revolutionary individualist must come the conserving community-ist. In place of the head-strong man of freedom must come the one who feels his life bound to Another who gives the freedom and the fellowship that really frees and gives mutual support. In place of the denominationalist must come *the* Church-man. In place of the philosopher of the Christian religion must come the Christian theologian. And by Christian theologian is meant the man of virile thought and action, whose motive, dynamic, and assumptions of thoughts start with God's action for man in Jesus Christ!

No church in America as presently constituted, or even inclined, can fulfill all these requirements. We can think of no new church that could be formed that would fulfill them. All human churches are relative and sinful. But there can develop and grow within all the present groups, which we now live in but do not assent to, a ferment of this new Church which shall inherit the future. This Church, within the churches, may not be able to fully articulate itself, but it can be the saving salt in the situation. It will not be a Church of any human reaction to the faith, but a Church of human beings who have a living theological stamina, whose lives are rooted in God in Christ and whose ethical credential is righteous love. Love will endure, and hope, and overcome all things, when grounded in the true purpose of life in God.

CHAPTER II

STERILE INTELLECTUALISM

CHRISTIANITY in America betrays a strong intellectual bent. (Paradoxically, we are theologically anaemic and intellectually active.) By that I mean we are in the throes of strong attempts to make Christianity reasonable. We will not exercise faith unless we can prove to ourselves whether or not a thing is true. We want to live by sight and not by faith. And this intellectual spirit is sterile!

Our whole temper since the founding of this republic has been pragmatic. We have so long lived intimately with *things* that we have the inveterate desire to make everything tangible and practical. We have seen so many impossibilities made possible in the physical world that we are skeptical of things that are beyond proof and manipulation.

There is a legitimate place for the use of reason in the Christian faith, but when reason becomes the sole criterion of judgment, faith is relegated to an insignificant place, and life takes on an aspect of coldness.

The term, "Oh, yeah?" is characteristic of our youth. It reveals a sly skepticism that doubts the unusual. A recent book title by Bruce Barton, *What Can a Man Believe?*[1] may reveal more than Mr. Barton would desire, for it makes faith a matter of

---

[1] Bobbs-Merrill Co., Indianapolis, Ind.

what a man *can* believe about God, not what a man *ought* to believe about God.

This-worldliness either breeds a religion of cold deism, or else plays into the hands of agnosticism, which is the final end of growing indifference.

Sincere critical realism may be helpful. But when it takes on absolute proportions, it may denature the imperatives of the gospel (which must be taken on faith), to the realm of the untenable, and hence irrelevant. We will need to rethink the relation of reason to revelation, to see that between true reason, that remains in its proper place, and revelation, that does not imply too much, there can be no disharmony.

Protestantism has always been a friend of reason. Despite the fact that Luther later distrusted it, nevertheless he and Calvin used reason in their monumental exegetical work; and, if we take reason in a larger sense, they used it in their search for God. But for Luther, a Christian's reasoning powers were free, yet paradoxically bound to God's Word in Christ. He conceived of faith as the higher reason, which leads the natural reason into fruitful fulfillment and creative intellectual pursuits. It was in bondage to the gospel, and that gave it its highest function. It was not sovereign, but under authority, under God. It operated in the narthex of reality, but was never able to enter the holy of holies of Reality. Reason could approach to, hint at, God, but never really know the Unknown God. It could serve the Word, but it could not produce it.

This is the early Protestant position as regards the intellect. Luther gave his intellect so much freedom, that it took the liberty to criticize the canon of Scriptures, saying that some parts of it were inferior in their revealing power of Christ, and that some were "right strawy." And he thought that extra-canonical literature, whether words of Pilate or of Satan, if it "themed" Christ, was authentic gospel. Calvin weighed the words of the Scriptures critically, and did not write a commentary on the book of Revelation.

The principle of individual freedom to search the Scriptures, of empirical scientific approach, of educational democracy, of a free critical spirit, is of the very essence of evangelical Christianity. The mind is valued, it is trusted, it is to be highly trained and developed, up to a certain point. It is no wonder that Protestantism has produced many of the modern philosophers of note, while Catholicism has not. Education for the masses, even in the coveted realms of higher culture, has followed in the wake of Protestant expansion. The ministry, except in some sects, has been fairly well trained in all branches of learning. Protestantism has nothing to fear from any of the positive contributions of humanism, modern science, philosophy, or psychology.

However, through the years, this rational tendency has been violently exaggerated by impetuous men. Not that they have emphasized this intellectual factor, but that they have neglected the "other" side of every perception and fact. The increasing emphasis upon the critical, the human, the empirical, and the obvious has blinded men to that "other" element that resides in, and yet is beyond, every phenomenon. For even about the "little flower in the crannied wall" there is a hidden sovereignty which is forever beyond the control of man's technique and the explanation of his mind. Some have gone so far as to deny the "other" element entirely. The weakness of this modern humanism is its tendency to forget that when it sets up its negative hypothesis it is using a fundamental, positive, "given" objective standpoint. Doubt is doubt because of the Great Affirmation! It is like a man denying the existence of the floor upon which he stands. The result is that what was meant to be a means, has been transferred to an end. In this respect the orthodox fundamentalist is equally at fault with his humanist brother. He too makes the humanly defined doctrine about Reality, which was meant to be a means, into an end which possesses a finality unwarranted in the face of the relativity of all human knowledge. In either case, the pride of human reason dissolves the fundamental ethical dualism of life. Such thinking is no longer reverent. Therein lies the problem of Protestant intellectualism.

The present "intellectual atmosphere," however, is rapidly taking on the air of humility. But there still exists in many quarters an unwarranted trust in the reason as the *only* and *authoritative* means for the discovery of God. An aristocracy of the intelligentsia is still threatening the foundations of Protestantism. The evangelical conception of a revealed gospel, the Word from and on God, as the central authority to which all men must anchor, is being threatened by an intellectualism which is dissolving every axiom of the faith. It has its vitiating effect upon pulpits and classrooms alike. This conclusion is inevitable if we grant the optimistic premise that the natural unaided intellect can find God and can know him by studying the world's behavior. This presupposes that there is no sin to blight the intellect, and, therefore, no need of a special revelation. As a result, Protestant Christianity becomes primarily intellectual.

This eliminates those who have not attended the graduate school. It makes God a matter of man's intellectual discussion. It results in a hesitancy to make a stand for the gospel. It ends in the vitiating *trek* and *search* for the truth. It makes of men mere spectators and connoisseurs in the realm of truth and God. It culminates in an ecclesiasticism of intellect as dogmatic as that of Middle-Age ecclesiasticism, or of seventeenth-century Protestant orthodoxy. Or it substitutes intellectual and logical consistency for ethical and religious righteousness. It saps religious vitality and ethical radicality. It levels and dilutes God and other objective verities to the level of the *possibility* of mental acceptance. It dissolves the dualism of God and man into an intellectual monism that is sterilizing in its effect on prayer, preaching, worship, art, and all phases of Christian truth. The needle's eye of Kingdom entrance is radically altered into the results of a syllogism, and the camels are the lowbrows! Such a Christianity dechristianizes uneducated people. It makes Christianity available only to a few, and places it in the straightjacket of *human rational* understanding.

Such intellectualism produces Pharisees and scribes, self-styled custodians of the wisdom of God. Man's mind becomes the measure of God. The commentator becomes master of the text; God the uncaused and unconditioned is helpless in the hands of his interpreters. The relativities of science are made into absolute dogmas. Sinful man's mind is the measure of truth!

Behind this sinister trend which has practically destroyed adventurous faith is the desire of the human to dodge his creaturehood and to usurp the rôle of master. It is intellectually humiliating to acknowledge that he does not know it all, and that he cannot scientifically control everything, even his ultimate destiny. To admit a world of unknown possibilities which have to be revealed to him, and which are beyond him, is to dissolve his pride. And that is demanding too much.

The truth is that modern science is not the culprit that has caused the dissolution of the distinction between God and the world. Rather, it is the human scientist himself who would rather play the master than the servant, the exhaustive explainer and controller than the disciple and the adjuster. Behind the uncritical monism of the day lies a moral problem. Man would rather see himself as good, as self-sufficient, than as basically sinful and dependent and in need of redemption from God.

This whole wave of radical analyses, characteristic of modern liberalism, is negative. It offers its contribution, of course, but it cannot *lead* us out into paths of dynamic living. It cannot arrive at a satisfying synthesis nor give positive, daring faith. This tendency has worked havoc in the higher grades of our public schools. Its worst effects have been felt in Christian, and other, colleges and universities, where professors have shocked student after student out of their orthodox home-training, and that of their local church. A modern equivalent was not even considered. Clever, smart, "half-baked" men who had had no contacts with life and its maturer responsibilities, or who were older and had avoided them— in the very halls built with contributions of the faithful common folk, turned out a host of youngsters who were nothing more than unprincipled sophists. Specialization, in an attempt to fulfill the intellectual standards set by the State, also contributed to this defection. Young preachers emerged from theological halls with a gospel of the interrogation point or a minimum "religion" of Christian veneered morals. This first consciousness of a freed intellect paved the way for a widespread agnosticism, skepticism, and cynicism, *the full effect of which we shall yet reap*.

Not all students nor all professors were such. Not all this sophistry was for naught. Iconoclasm has its merit. It liquidates the watered stock of non-productive life and reveals frozen assets. It tests the actual usable capital of any age. Destructive criticism may whet the forces of construction; it may clear the wilderness for the coming of a greater glory.

When intellect becomes an end instead of a means, however, it results in an egotism far more sinister and subtle than the egotism of physical power. Ultimately this intellectualism fails, flounders, and ends in either stern stoicism or futile cynicism. This element of superiority is more strongly pronounced in younger scholars than we realize. The Athenian élite is an individualist, and is apt to draw off from mankind's common ills in a monastic caste. Especially is that true if the institution in which he teaches is supported by an endowment, thus making it unnecessary to appeal to the constituency which built it. Then an aristocracy develops which is far removed from life, and which esoterically forgets the average man. This atmosphere lurks on every campus of size and remains with many a graduate after his departure. Intellectualism does that if it is not hitched to the meaningfulness of life in God. It is Protestantism's prodigal child!

This intellectual drift within Protestantism has gone so far that it has become stale. A dark and impenetrable cloud seems to have settled upon the intellectuals. A frigid paralysis is evident. Intellectualism has no power to save itself. It has gone to seed. It has lost its Master, its sense of mission. In the modern crises of life its method of arriving at any fortifying help from the beyond has been sterile.

Its inquiry into the biblical narratives, the person of Jesus, or Paul, the rise of the early Church, and kindred realms, has failed to answer any of our urgent questions with positive conviction. It has missed the main point in its analysis of the Bible. Its alliance with modern philosophy and psychology has been detrimental. In fact, instead of exclamation points we are confronted with larger question marks. It has been destructive of the cardinal fact of Protestantism; it has practically displaced two things: faith as a technique for discovering God, and God's radical revelation in Christ. With a cynical smile, it has murdered revelation in cold blood, and has triumphantly "explained away" what it has destroyed. By its thoroughgoing empiricism and attendant monism it has forgotten or lost the need for the gospel. It works havoc with the preacher in the pulpit!

What is more, its desire to make Christianity respectable to the modern intellect as the criterion of truth-judgment has diluted the religion of the campus and of a generation of graduates down to something negligible, problematical, or irrelevant. If the campus is sadly lacking in the radical Christian gospel at its very core of group life, one reason may be that the gospel has been forced to take its place with other subjects as a questionable and shifting science, or philosophy. When the Christian gospel and its product, Christian ethics, become a science, or even a "religion" alongside of others, they are no longer what original and early Protestantism claimed for them. The gospel is not a science, nor is it a system of technical metaphysics. It is an absolute norm of God, an act and offer of God that does not depend upon science, philosophy, or any other human discipline, and as such is never in disagreement with true science and the humble intellect. In its simplicity it rests upon the very poles of universal existence: the ethical natures of God and man, as revealed in the Word of God.

Certainly Christian theology, as historically formulated, is a shifting science. Let the intellect formulate as best it can these peripheral questions about ecclesiastical organization, doctrinal formulation, and the subsidiary questions concerning the origin and structure of society and the world. The Protestant intellect must always be free. But it can never enter the portals of the gospel of God, which tells of God's sovereign moral judgment, God's love-call to men, His ethical demands, His purpose, His coming to men, His demand for surrender to His redeeming love. In this realm faith and revelation are supreme. Man's mind cannot *create* these. The soil cannot create the seed, nor the dough the leaven. And faith is a life-qualifier. It is not meant to explain everything. Faith is the responsive adventure of the essential man. And revelation is God's act, in which He shares His purpose with men who by their very sin have lost His way.

Intellectualism has often confused the gospel, which never varies, with the historical accidents of the gospel in various ages. Many have thought of the gospel as no longer potent in our age, because they have been able to "explain" some of the Bible as prescientific and hence no longer tenable. But this does not invalidate the gospel. Many of our modern books have sought to explain the Bible and certain aspects of Christian history to the modern mind. Many of these attempts have not furthered the cause, nor made the power of Christianity work today, largely because too much emphasis was laid upon the negative aspects of the "explanation."

Surely, there are many things about the Bible and Christian history that we cannot hold today. Surely, the clothing in which the gospel was dressed needs to be replaced with modern thought-forms. But let there be no confusion on the point that to change the dress of the gospel does not mean *that the gospel itself is invalidated*. Our intellectual attempts, for instance, to explain the substitutionary idea of the atonement of Anselm in the light of the feudal relations of Anselm's age, do not for a single moment invalidate the truth beneath the idea by which thousands have lived and died. And the inherent and constant reality in Anselm is not to be dismissed because we in a superior attitude "understand" the age of Anselm. The same is true of many phases of the Bible. The gospel has to do with the moral existence of man and not with the accidentals of life in which he lives. Often intellectualism is only a form of the pride of man which hopes that by explaining something its reality no longer has sovereign power over him.

Only an intellectual maturity on the part of our Protestant leaders can suffice here. The intellectuals will have to vacate their throne. *But*, they need not get off the field. Yet, we will have to cease worshiping their academic wares. Protestant scholarship must go *through* the modern temper to the original Protestant or historic evangelical position: the reason must have its full freedom, provided it is in bondage to the simple objective gospel of God. And that gospel is simpler than ecclesiastics and theologians have said it is. We will need to become more desperate about God and the logic of life than about intellectual consistency and the logic of the schools. The difficulty is that we have lost the divine compulsion of our ethical gospel that is addressed to all men. A period of searing and consuming criticism will assist to bring it to the fore. We are too much at home in our intellectual haven, around which there is usually a thick shell of pride of achievement. All this must be eliminated, this "slum at the top," before the Spirit of God can come with terrific power.

A great deal of significance must be attached to recent developments in the field of philosophy, theology, and science, which are evidently rehabilitating theism. Physics and astronomy, as well as biology, are recognizing the fallibility of the mechanico-physical theory of the universe and life. Of greater significance is the phenomenological movement, so closely associated with Professor Edmund Husserl, of Germany. It is winning adherents in the

United States. Similar trends toward a newer objectivity are noticeable in some quarters, independent of Husserl. This movement does not discard psychology, but, by means of it, seeks to discover the objective world in and yet beyond man. By "bracketing" all psychophysical aspects of the experience through reflection, it eliminates all but that which belongs to pure essence. Thus they hope to arrive at the Objective without recourse to an *a priori* dogmatic statement of it. They discover the Unconditioned Reality in all things. They are valuable allies in the rehabilitation of theism. It is an omen of the return of a transcendent element in the self. Christian scholars can rejoice in phenomenology, providing they do not depend upon it for *their knowledge of the ethical nature of ultimate Truth.*[2]

Another omen is the increasing rise of irrationalism in many forms. It is found in literature, and since literature has always been an index to the current thinking of any age, it is significant and revealing. Even cynicism is a form of irrationalism, as is much of modern humanism. But in philosophy it is most pronounced in some mathematicians. The whole trend indicates the rising distrust of the rational powers exhaustively to explain phenomena. The truth beyond irrationalism is that subjects are not only "taught," but that the reality of them must be "caught." Phenomena contain something that is finally incommunicable and indescribable. It may be

---

[2] The Christian gospel is not philosophical theism!

possible to convey certain relations and connections, but the actual feeling-tone, "intention"—(while we may talk about it, it is not to be identified with our talk)—the "tone" of the phenomenon is always beyond us, incapable of control, it is sovereign. There is a terrible privacy about the least of things. And that privacy is most terrible in God, in Jesus. The *a priori* is coming back, and with it the soul, the self!

These movements are symptomatic of the stalemate in intellectual pursuits which seems to focus in psychology. The end has been an overdevelopment of method at the expense of reality and essence. They are an indication of the approaching sterility of pure humanistic immanence, of scientific dogmatism, unless redeemed by a correspondingly intense transcendence.

But this method does not go far enough to give us saving and satisfying Truth. It never gets beyond the *spectator's* position as regards God's nature. It does not get beyond the human possibility of discovery. It discovers an inescapable fact of the "unknown" God present in, and beyond, the objects of life. It discovers the vast Substratum, the Foundation, of all existence. It rehabilitates the purposive design, and integration principle, of the world. But it cannot get through to *it*, to find out its nature. It stands at the gates of reality but never enters. It cannot. But it stands upon the threshold in a reverent wonder. It gives us clues as to the Object's behavior, but that behavior cannot be discovered with any degree of finality so as to give warrant for personal decision and ethical action. That requires personal, God-sharing, unique *revelation*.

It falls short in the most important field of personal life and destiny. To be a mere spectator means that one never enters the fray. He remains outside. If we are to have saving Truth, we must not merely look at it, but it must look at us. The Object must probe and question us. It must become personal; it must speak. To do that it must have ethical character and personality. And it must reveal itself in a personal way. This the Object of philosophy and science does not possess, and if their adherents say "It" does, they are exceeding their bounds as spectators. Intellectualism thus assists—but it never leads to God the Father, holy and righteous, yet full of *love*. Its logic never undergirds its ethics with religious passion.

We must make very clear the difference between two types of thinking—the theoretical and the existential. Christianity in a real sense is not theoretical and rational, it has always been "existential."

Theoretical thinking is observatory. It stands apart and seeks rationally to explain the "how" and the "why" of an event—which is not the most important thing about the event. This sort of thinking is fragmentary, because it utilizes only a part of the human personality—the rational. It plays the part of a spectator.

Professor William Lyon Phelps gives an interesting illustration from literature that describes the

difference between these two types of thinking. He
shows that existential thinking is living, and never
static. It is youthful and never aged. He shows
how the literati have treated the narrative of Jesus'
raising of Lazarus from the grave. Most of them
deal with the "how" of the event, or with the problem of *where* Lazarus was during the days of his
death. It was not until Browning appeared, says
Professor Phelps, that the reality of the event found
expression in poetry. Browning caught the functional and living truth of it when he interpreted it
in terms of the change it made in the lives of those
who contemplated and watched the event.

In short, those who participated in the life of the
event were thinking existentially. For existential
thinking means that the whole person enters, is
drawn into, the event it seeks to understand. It lets
itself be drawn into the moving and forming factors
of the deed. It utilizes the high powers of moral
imagination, spiritual insight, and repentant, recep-
tive faith. It does not stop with the mere human
idea of a thing, nor with the dogma about it, but is
concerned with the thing itself, its reality and its
sovereign life. Never does existential thinking seek
exhaustively and rationally to control the object of
its study. On the contrary, it allows the thing
studied to study the observer. Never does existential thinking involve only the *human* understanding
of God; it lets God give a divine understanding of
man the thinker. It is not fragmentary thinking,
done for the mere amusement of research. The

whole man enters into the knowing act with a desperate desire to be researched, or "placed," himself.[3]

Christianity is a religion of existential thinking. It is different from all other religions in this respect. The New Testament proves this throughout. How different it is from any other religious literature! And Jesus Christ? While there is much about Him that can be rationally understood, yet the most important thing about Him is His power to find man, to reach his real problem of existence, which is moral guilt; to face man with the qualitative character-reality of man, as well as of God. He is always intent upon revealing the real problem (crisis) of human life. No dispenser of wisdom is Jesus! No philosopher of the *a priori* is Jesus. *He finds and redeems sinners.*

Christianity is not the revelation of a detailed *system* of philosophical metaphysics, nor of a theory of the world's origin, nor of a theory of social organization, nor even of an ethical code of conduct. Christianity is the revelation of the nature and purpose and love and will of God and the real nature of man. As such it can never be purely theoretical reason, which shifts with varying age and comes into every increasing fact of scientific knowledge. Jesus Christ brings us no new rational knowledge. He faces us directly with the natures of God and man, which are never capable of theoretical knowledge. Only existentially are they made known by those

---

[3] Modern American thought as seen in amusement life, academic life, has been highly spectative, not participative.

who in obedient faith follow the real Jesus. The whole Bible is realistic in its thinking. Faith is the highest rational technique for the knowledge of God. It involves the whole man with his entire make-up as an ethical personality. Failure to see this, makes our highly enlightened age so sterile in divine action. Our thinking must become more passionate.

As stated once before, the reason we do not know God more vitally and dynamically today is not because modern science makes it impossible. Nor because we do not possess enough knowledge. It is because we have dissolved everything to the plane of the natural, because we do not like to have anything beyond and above us. It is too humiliating! We do not like to admit that our intellectual capacities as such are not enough to lead us to a saving knowledge of God. We like to "go it" alone. Faith is seemingly so humiliating. We are too proud of our orthodoxies, both liberal and conservative. We do not like to confess that even our ideas, our theologies, our dogmas, are relative; that they are merely passing techniques and frameworks that shall pass away, even as heaven and earth.

This does not crucify reason. On the contrary, faith completes reason. It glorifies reason with its true function. It is not without wonder that the humble and obedient faithful have possessed powers of sustained reasoning that have baffled philosophy. Faith releases the true character of reason to its highest powers. It integrates life around its true goal.

It is well to remember that prophets seldom emerge from schools of philosophy or ethics—or from theological seminaries. John the Baptists seldom come from Jerusalems. And Sauls have to lay aside all attempts at vain philosophy (scientific theism) and rabbinism (ethical theism) and count these as refuse, after years of reconstruction in Arabian and Tarsusian isolation, before they become flaming apostles of God. Here is Protestantism's solution to its enervating intellectualism. It is in a new spirit rather than a new system.

In closing this brief chapter it must be said that a mere going "one step farther" in our present Protestant intellectual situation is not enough. True, there is a way of going *through* science to the object of life. No intensification of the human intellect, however, will ever give birth to the idea of the Fatherhood of God as revealed in the Word of God.[4]

In this respect American liberal theology is not enough. It still hopes through its intellectualism to come to some sort of Christian Reality. This method, in the end, betrays itself in any case into a higher type of rationalism. There is still too much optimism in the modern attempts at a scientific theism, optimism as to the power of the rational capacities of man actually to discover "pure" data as regards God in the human religious consciousness. It ignores the whole realm of sin and that of reli-

---

[4] Making man's mind keener will not create the knowledge of God that saves.

gious epistemology—which cannot be ignored. And it certainly ignores the whole basis of New-Testament faith. It still seeks religious Reality on the basis of the old intellectualism. In this respect the Greeks and Hindus have done all the thinking that can be done. It is the opinion of the writer that all such attempts will fail to reach that power of Reality which we find in the New-Testament faith and in the virile life of the historic Church. We must come to a new way of thinking, we must be done with this cautious rationalistic intellectualism, and must come to the existential type of thinking which produces faith. For faith is the only method that discovers the Christian realities. In the chaos of the modern world and its muddled and diversified thought we should see that all man's thinking about the Reality of God and life is colored with a thick mist of something the ancients called sin. Otherwise we would have had unity of thought about God ever since the Greeks. We need revelation. *God* must speak to us; *He must reveal Himself*. This is *the* need of which modern intellectualism is not yet conscious. And that is why so much of it is sterile—and verbose. For the Christian, God is anything but a datum of natural science discoverable by the pure intellect.

Cautious intellectualism will never give birth that faith in God which comes of a God who apprehends men in spite of their failure to have a consistent intellectual philosophy. This age is hungry for a faith in something beyond its power to verify with logic. It desires a life of high meaning, the following of which releases and empowers and fortifies and enhopes with an eternal meaningfulness.

Even a proud intellectualism must be counted as "loss" for the more "excellent knowledge" of Jesus Christ. When our thinkers reach that stage, there will be a rebirth of real, living Christian theology.

CHAPTER III

CHRISTIANITY TOO "RELIGIOUS"

THE Christianity of our churches is far too "religious"! Such a statement may sound strange to the reader. We have always associated "religion" with the higher aspirations of man.

"Religion" has its legitimate place. But "religiousness" is, after all, a hazy thing. All men are "religious" in the sense that they live by something that directs their lives and guides their ambitions. All men have in their hearts secret shrines to some object of trust that is other than God. It may be an ambition that is no higher than "man at his best." But such "religious" men are not necessarily Christian.

"Religion" is an uncertain term; it may mean anything to anyone. In that sense our churches are too "religious." "Religion" too usually refers to "religious" practices of men. The effects upon a person as he comes in contact with the object of his religious faith are often termed the criteria by which we judge whether one is "religious" or not. If a man goes through the forms of prayer, the form of churchgoing, the form of benevolence, the form of conversion, we often think him "religious." This sort of judgment is, after all, a "religious" judgment on man. These effects may have their value as "fruits" of the "religious" life. But "religious"

60

fruits do not alone determine whether or not one is a Christian.

In this sense our American churches are too "religious." They are bent more on producing the secondary effects of "religious life" than in emphasizing the primary objects of faith that originate, feed, and sustain the Christian Way of life.

There is a great deal of interest in "religion" in America. If we are to believe our librarians, "religious" books are widely and voluminously read. Perhaps it is this very "religiousness" that makes God so indefinite a quantity and so ineffective a reality in our modern world.

The difficulty is that "religion" means so many things to so many people. "Religion" is something people may speak about glibly and speculatively. One may even play at "being religious." It may be "quite interesting." Often, the terms "religion" and "Church" mean one and the same thing. In that case we think of the task of the Church and the nature of Christianity as identical with a general form of "religion."

To avoid any misunderstanding it is essential that the reader know definitely what is meant by the term "religion" and the term "revelation," as used in this chapter. "Religion" is the attempt on man's part to build up a satisfying system and philosophy of thought, action, or feeling on the basis of an interpretation of his environment and intuitions. In short, it is an exalted human man-made philosophy of life which man invents and lives by, whereby he hopes to give his life high meaning. "Religion" is what man finally thinks about his life and destiny on the basis of his own thought. As such, "religion" is common to all men.

"Revelation," on the contrary, is something basic and peculiar to Christianity. It is not a man-invented interpretation of life and destiny, but an objective presentation from God of a hope, a command, a purpose which comes to man from outside and beyond himself. It is a new beginning in God. It is God's opening of a new Way unto Himself. This revelation does not give man detailed scientific knowledge; it, rather, offers man that which can save him from frustration, meaninglessness, defeat, limitation, and sin. Revelation is the sovereign declaration of God to man of His purpose, His authority, and His love. Such revelation is anything but "religion." (But man often makes revelation into "religion"!)

Revelation is not common to all men. "Religion" is man's common quest for God. Christian faith rests upon God's revealing Himself to man! Much that is today regarded as Christianity is nothing more than a human "religious interest" in the problems of life. Christianity in many churches has been emasculated of its faith-content. An extravagant optimism has made the need for revelation unnecessary, and as a result Christianity is regarded as a cultivation of high human aspirations, or as conclusions of the mind about nature and human intuitions. The heart of Christianity once was "to glorify God." Today it is hardly more than the development of human life to a point of inner satisfaction or outer respectability. The radical element in the Christian tradition has been toned down to a place where it no longer judges or challenges man from a superhuman plane. Therefore, we speak of modern Christianity as "religious," as a human "religiousness," hardly to be distinguished from a high human ethics or philosophy. But that is certainly not faith in the real God who is beyond our interpretation, the God whom Christianity in its virile days always believed to have revealed Himself in an authoritative, definite, and authentic way.

Modern Protestantism is chaotic, due not to the economic situation but to too much "religion," which is hardly more than the bedlam of thousands of "religions" in conflict. This is the incipient chaos of modern life. It is at the heart of our denominational confusion. To our fathers the Word of God was no such indefinite and hazy "religious" individualism. To them, the Word was neither material fetish nor the changing word of man written in large letters. It was the arresting emergence of the eternal in time, and it confronted man not as the basis of a human "religion," but as the only starting point of a God-meaningfulness which man could never discover in his lostness. This Word was not the basis of a human "religion." It was mediated only through the Scriptures, specifically through Jesus Christ and historically through the Church of a true witness and faith.

There was a time when Christianity was everywhere considered a unique revelation, and when all other religions were looked upon as "pagan" or "heathen." It was regarded as *the* way, *the* truth and *the* life, different not only in *degree* but in *kind* from all other religions. Increasingly in modern times, this view has been modified or even surrendered. In orthodox circles it is still held, but in liberal circles it has been greatly modified so that Christianity is considered to be the highest and best form of general "religion," not unlike other religions in *kind*. Some have even gone so far as to regard elements in other religions as superior to Christianity.

But even in orthodox circles, other religions are not regarded as machinations of the devil. In the medieval age it was considered meritorious to burn or torture heretics, and to forcibly convert the "heathen." In any case, even the orthodox will admit that other religions have beneath them a deep desire to know the meaning of life. All religions seek in one way or another to give life a divine meaningfulness, to give high sanction to life's actions, to provide life with fortifications in the face of changing scenes, and a hope and an end in the midst of life's inevitable frustrations. In truth, they all seek to put their adherents in proper relation to the "Determiner of destiny." In a real sense we are not speaking of the inner meaning in other religions. We are speaking of the modern word used in church circles, called "religion."

In the course of time this high conception of the

absoluteness and "onlyness" of Christianity was affected by many currents of modern thought and life. The study of other religions by scientific scholars revealed the sincere faith of their adherents. Some of the teachings of Jesus and the prophets were found in the teachings of other religious sages. Beneath other religions they discovered a deep general hunger for superhuman supports of life. They possessed some idea of the reality of life's frustration due to evil, which required some kind of atonement. They also possessed priests and teachers, religious dogmas, temples, prayer rituals, objects of adoration, and religious psychological reactions that appeared like those which Christianity possessed. As a result, changes came in the interpretation of Christianity in relation to other religions. Finally, scholars came to the conclusion that Christianity was, after all, *one* of the religions of the world. It was like other religions, but it differed from them in degree. It was "Religion" itself, a quintessence of all that was best in every religion. The psychology, philosophy, sociology, and history of religion came in to support these conclusions.

Of course, other factors were involved in this process of making Christianity into a "religion" among others. People began to travel and thereby to broaden their sympathies. They noticed that there were good, pious, sincere, and intellectual people among the so-called "heathen" religions.

Further, the rise of this-worldliness made Christianity's appeal to an other-worldly revelation seem anachronistic. Even Christianity began to apologize for the audacity of its claim to revelation, and scholars soon found a way of "explaining" the elements of Christianity in purely historical, subjective, social, and psychological ways. Besides, other religions claimed to have revelations too, as well as sacred books and infallible dogmas. The functions of sacrifice and prayer and priestly meditation seemed to be identical with those practiced by Christians.

With the rise of the idea that religion originated in, and was native to, man's religious consciousness, it became the accepted custom of Christian scholars to admit that all religions arose in the souls of men in similar fashion the world over. Thus, Christianity originated in Judaism, and Judaism received most of its religious ideas and ideals from neighboring nations and its own environment. Jesus' ideas, as well as those of the prophets, were, after all, those of highly gifted geniuses, whose sensitivity of spirit made it possible for them to enunciate the highest discoverable religious truths latent in all other religious or philosophic quests.

Philosophers, too, turned their thoughts from theology as a science of a given revelation, and began to seek truth inductively within man. "Religion" in time became the highest kind of philosophy, a philosophy in which men found an adequate and satisfying explanation and synthesis of life on the basis of a study of nature and the intuitions of man. Christianity was incorporated into this scheme. Man, it was held, is normally endowed with something divine, an innate divinity, the arousal and development of which is the task of all religions, but that through the pattern of Jesus we are able to attain the highest human development. *Christian absolutes were thereby relativized.*

Such an interpretation, it is true, put a premium upon natural and normal human life. It did help to rightfully redeem man from utter depravity by making him a potential son of God.

But it went too far. In the end, Christian faith became a "religion," or "*the* Religion." (In fact, the Judaism of Jesus' day had become such a program and plan of "religion" and self-culture. And the making of Christianity into a "religion" has been frequently done in the history of the Church.) When that happens, a very important thing takes place—the very core of the Christian faith is changed from a revealed truth which comes into the world and to which men are called, into a *religiousness* of life. Such religiousness may even produce aesthetic worship, good deeds, and ethical action. Faith in something not naturally human is altered into a cultivation of a quality of life for its own sake.

One can easily see how this transition of Christian faith in Christ as the absolute Son of God into a "religion of man," who, with the help of God (who is interpreted in many forms from sacred literature to sunsets!) *makes himself religious.* Thus Christianity becomes like an art. It becomes a religion, or even "*the* Religion," of man.

Perhaps we should clarify the issues somewhat

more fully. The modern man uses the word "religion" far more than he uses the word "God." In short, he is thinking more of general, subjective "religion" than of the definite, objective God-reality of Christianity. He is thinking mostly of the *forms* of religion in general, or of the *effects* of religiousness in good feeling, moral action, or intellectual dogmas. Or, he is thinking about interesting "religious" ideas. He may even be thinking of "religion" in universal terms, as that syncretism of all religions into a great religion of the world.

But is his thinking critical and right? Can there ever be such a thing as a universal religion of man concocted out of all the good elements of every religion? The fact of the matter is that *all* religions are local, and to take the most important elements out of their local context would be to break down their structures. Most religions are ethnic, national or local. Therein they are strong! And even if we succeeded in getting all good elements into a religion, would there be any agreement as to what sort of an organism that would make? There would still be vagueness, because, after all, each philosopher, and each psychologist of religion would have "his own religion." Besides, such a syncretistic religion would be only another religion among others. Religion would still be a subjective thing, common, it is true, to all men, but having no objective power of truth.

One could not even include Buddhism and Hinduism in the same religion, for the strength of

Buddhism is in its denial of God, and the strength of Hinduism is in the fanatical affirmation of manifold gods. In fact, there can never be such a thing as "religion." Is Christianity, therefore, a "religion," after all?

Perhaps the modern man has lost faith in other-worldly absolutes. It is not entirely his fault. Yet, he sets up *his own* absolutes on the basis of science and constructs a "religion" for himself from the facts of human life and history. So every man has a "religion," whether he denies the existence of other absolutes or not. But is his "religion" right? Or is it what true "religion" should be to all men? Is such a "religion" Christian?

For us who call ourselves Christians there has come a definite insecurity regarding Christianity conceived as merely "religion." The word "religion," as applied to Christianity, means too many things to too many people. It does not seem to harmonize with a persistent absolutism which has inhered in our historic faith. It does not seem even "scientifically" correct to classify Jesus with religious "geniuses." He cannot be placed on a plane with a genius. The reality with which Jesus confronts us does not seem, even in kind, to be like that which we confront in any other religion. Christ meets man "head-on," and not in a way to enthrone man. The stark reality of Christianity does not at all reside in its power to make men "religious." It resides, rather, in its power to make men realists, to relate them to God, who does not enhance man, but who apprehends and saves and empowers the natural man from outside man.

There is also a universal element in Christianity which does not die, but which survives transplantation to other cultures and races and ages. The God of Christian faith is hardly to be compared with Hindu gods, or Buddhistic nihilism, or the central reality of any other religion. Christianity's God is personal and ethical. He reveals himself in self-movement toward man. The Christian God of revelation is not a provincial Deity. He is Lord.

The Christian gospel demands response and decision. There is nothing in the New Testament to indicate that man must "religiously" climb to heaven to bring God down. Rather, it speaks of a revealing God who comes to man to save man where he is. Christianity is not a refined self-salvation. It creates a ferment at the heart of its disciples. It is born in high personal decision. Christianity does not lull to sleep in mysticism; it does not consist of cold ethical principles; nor does its power inhere in intellectual expertness. There seems to be no scientific way of proving the nature of its central revealed truth, for it stands in its own right, and has emerged without the thinking of man in "religious" quest. The Christ meets us like a rising sun.

Christianity is not "religion," hazy and uncertain; it is a definite faith in a definite Person, who comes to us from beyond our intuitions and the natural habits of nature. At the heart of Christianity is an Absolute.

"Religion" has no need to defend itself against rational attack. It can be manipulated by men—yes, even changed. Christianity, however, is open to rational attack, because it contradicts rational truth. It cannot be manipulated; it is sovereign. "Religion" has to do with the subjective; Christian faith has to do with trust in a self-revealing objective reality. Therefore, Christianity cannot be understood merely from the standpoint of psychology or history. "Religion" may produce worship, but faith produces always a living, personal theology. True, there are "religious" elements in Christian faith, and it does express itself in such human reactions. But the human expressions are secondary. Other "religions" can out-do Christianity in cult, mysticism, ethicism, formalism—in all that pertains to "religion." But they lack the "one thing needful."

The very substitution of the word "religion" for Christian "faith" reveals that fundamental sin of man which does not care to find life in dependence upon Another. Man would rather live by a "religion" of his own creation. And modern Christianity is tainted with the autonomous desire of man to live without revelation, or the necessity of revelation. Witness the pride of the modern Church, its feverish activity and desire for power, its unconcern for sound knowledge.

Such terms as the "revival of religion" and a "revealed religion" are absurd. No "religion" is ever revealed. And as for the "revival" of religion, that is a comparatively easy task. The revival of piosity, of moral fervency, and of intellectual concern for "religiousness" is not difficult, but it is all so futile and meaningless. Far more important is it to recognize, to be obedient to, and to glorify God. Even the term "Christianity" is misleading. It sounds like a human manipulation of the divine. Calvin used the word "religion" in his title to the *Institutes,* but he had no idea the word would be so commonly used, nor that it would be confused with the essence of the Christian faith.

Christian faith in God is something quite different from mere "religiosity." The latter is something all-too-human. It stands for the divinized natural man, the godly Pharisee, the decent churchman, the moral and dogmatic man. How often have Continentals spoken of the *"geistlichen,"* the clericals, the spiritual *bourgeois* custodians of "religion," as though "religion" were a possession of man, a something which he could boast about and improve himself with, to the humiliation of his fellows. Let the world ridicule the so-called "clergy" who presume to have a "corner" on God. We do too! When men think of the Christian God, or the Christian faith, in terms of human possessions, they have made of God and the faith—a human "religion."

If "religion" means to possess a divine something in the soul; if it means to become peculiar in the sense of differentness from other men; if it stands for that possessive spirit which struts through the earth viewing men from a superior pharisaical moral or intellectual or emotional plane; if it makes natural man to pride himself on what he has done to lift himself to the throne of God, then such "religion" is *not* Christianity. In its essence Christianity is the direct opposite.

With such a spirit Jesus had nothing to do. To be born again means for man to be completely divested of his "religion." Man is a sinner and as such has to be *completely* helped, not merely assisted by a God who allows man to usurp the throne. Jesus would never countenance a "religion" that ends in mere intensified religious feeling, in intellectual acumen, in ethical action. There were plenty of such religious tendencies in his day. All these helped to crucify him. What Jesus brought to the world was a God-realism and a man-realism that destroy man's pride and exalt the reality of God. He did not come to give *man* a "religion" that would make *man* feel good, or that would result in personal prosperity. He came to declare *the* Truth, to incarnate it in flesh and blood.

Jesus had little to do with "religion." He is not like any of the founders of other religions. He is lowly, He refuses earthly pomp, and His power does not reside in His religious practices but in His humility and obedience. God was Lord through Jesus. Jesus was not full of divine godliness. He has nothing about Him of a "quester," helping *man to* God. For Jesus, God comes to man. His "religion," if such it may be called, is fact and life and way and truth. The uniqueness of Christianity is in its content and not in its religiosity.

There is a reason why the disciples were called Christians, and not adherents of the Christian "religion." Christians have no "religion"; they are Christ-men and Christ-women. Perhaps along this line lies our pathway to a united Christian strength. Christian faith is expressed in varied forms, but *the* faith is the same. Let there be no confusion of "Christian faith" with the "religious," or "denominational," elements in that faith. (If the Roman Catholic allows his "religious" symbols and his various means of Christian worship to remain secondary aid in their places, we have no quarrel with him, his fellows, his crosses, his masses.)

Nor will it be necessary for Oriental Christians to discard their religious customs if they can be used with new Christian meanings. Always the faith must keep a critical eye upon the "religious" expressions of that faith, and allow the Truth of Christian faith to maintain its sovereignty. As such, nothing human will be alien to the mastery of faith, and the Christian's lot will be cast in the midst of his earthly life so that his family life, his vocation, and all that is human, while always relative and sinful, can have a sacramental meaning. The Christian is not a humanistic theocentrist, but a theocentric humanist. He lives by revelation, namely, God's mercy and sharing grace, and not by *his* highest "religious" aspirations. His faith will not be an "opiate" for his bad situation, but a power for the redemption of, and in, his situation. It will provide him with a new fulcrum of divine meaningfulness that is not at the mercy of changing mental and social states. His life will be rooted and grounded in the Living God.

The Object of his faith will be not only the realistic evaluator of his sinfulness which deserves righteous condemnation, but also the only reason for his ability to affirm life in the love and hope of God. The Christian's faith is anything but a "religious culture." It is, rather, a declaration of truth and God. God will have reached down into his life to make it possible for him to live at all.

Donald Lowrie in his excellent book, *Religion or Faith*, to which this chapter owes a great debt, says that the conflict of the early Church with other religions was not a conflict of "religions," Christianity included. It was a conflict of human "religion" against Christian "faith." Christian faith on the defensive was intolerant, but not with the intolerance of a medieval Church and its materialistic concept of the Church. It staked its all on the objective power of its faith-object. "Religions" are usually tolerant, but virile Christianity by its very nature is intolerant, not in its human aspect but in its very content. Wherever Christ is truly preached, a conflict takes place. There the demons begin to sense a battle! "Religion" belongs to the realm of this "world," and it rises up against the absolute reality of Christ, who always strikes at its assumed false sovereignties and seeks to dethrone them.

The strength of evangelical Christian realism will be determined largely by its divorce from "religion." To be true to itself it must leave the questionable comforts, the pomp and the prestige that "religion" gives and stake its all on the pilgrim's path as an obedient *witness* to truth and God. All too long has the glib and cultured talk of "religion" been a mere alibi, enabling man to cloak his self-esteem under the cloak of religiosity. God in Christ tears off that cloak, places man in the category of the sinner that he is and tells him his only hope is in service and dependence upon the grace of his God.

To let God do this will be a herculean task. For the modern man has accustomed himself to think solely in terms of time, until he thinks even of God as a great Man, or of the Word of God as the word of man spoken loudly, or of eternity as infinitely elongated time, or of the kingdom of God as an intensified and goodly human world.

It is not "religion" that we lack. There is all too much of it abroad in the earth. It is rampant in the Church. Even the Christian "religion" must be destroyed! We lack God, the real God, who has the power to humble us to the dust and make us take our lives again from His extended loving hand. Such a faith would move mountains; such a faith could revitalize the Church; such a faith would provide a channel for some small measure of eternal power to flow into our world, through human obedience. It would not completely save the world, but it would salt it, illumine it, and leaven it with that which would qualify a world that is fast on its way to disintegration—even in its "religiousness" and its "religious interest."

The real heart of Christianity is not so much historical, scientific, or social knowledge. Man can discover these by his own capacities, unaided. The message of the gospel does not teach men something they do not know in the realm of agriculture, physics, or history. The gospel is not a supernatural packet of mysterious knowledge which God gives to man in the infallible language of the Bible. The message of Christianity is neither a philosophical nor a sociological, nor even a theological system. The Christian message does not explain everything. Rather, it is a qualifying message—a call, a command, a promise, a purpose. And the one who responds to this gospel of God works at his science, his history, his agriculture, and the normal pursuits of life in a new spirit of faith and hope. This message is addressed to the essential man from God. It calls the total man to active response.

Thus the gospel message does not unfit one for life's normal pursuits. Rather, it undergirds one's work with a qualifying purpose which asks repentance of men. Nor does the gospel message operate only in restricted areas of life; it is meant to qualify the lives of all men. The gospel is a power from God in life. All other forms of high and noble knowledge lack this good news, this passion of life that is born of God's initiative and not of man's intuition and self-culture.

Much high and admirable moral and religious knowledge has been discovered by man in his long history. Through an interpretation of nature about

him and his intuitions within him he has amassed a
great deal of classical wisdom, even religious love.
But such "religion" does not reveal a gospel of good
news. Most of it issues from a cool observation of
the world without and within, from the point of view
of a spectator. It leaves man just where he is. Man
may have a deep sense of reverence within him in
the face of the vast universe, a feeling of the awfulness of its mystery. He may, like Plato, come to a
sense of the beauty, goodness, and truth of the
Supreme Being in the universe. He may even speak
of virtue as the highest characteristic of man's nobility. He may arrive at the knowledge that goodness,
beauty, and truth are the highest ends of man.

Yet all these are a long way from the simple gospel of Christianity, which is founded, not in cool cal-
culation, but in joyous discovery of God's revelation
to man of His love and His purpose and His call.
There is a vast difference between the highest humanistic religious achievement and the Christian
reality of the incarnate love of God. The former is
based upon what *man does for himself,* the other is
based upon what *God does for man.* One can easily
understand why the gospel is "foolishness" to the
Greek philosopher, and a "stumbling-block" to the
Jewish moralist. Both are humanists! The Christian is anything but a religionist. He is a biblical,
or Christ, realist. He starts with God's act which
meets him in the story beneath the Bible records.

To sum up: the Church is faced with a sinister
enemy in the very secularism which it sanctioned in

the name of liberalism. For the Christian core of reality has been diluted to harmonize with the dominant ideas of nineteenth-century monistic science. It was even urged that Christianity should relate itself more closely to the so-called "religious" desires of the whole world. Christian "revelation" was thereby abandoned in favor of a general "religion" in which God was manifesting Himself all the time. The whole history of "religion" was regarded as a process of evolutionary progressive revelation. Thus Christianity was fitted into a scheme of general world "religion." The difference between "religion" in general and Christian "revelation" then became negligible. Much of our decline in missionary urgency is due to this loss of a clear distinction between "religion" and the Christian gospel, in which God actually imparts His will to men. As a result, Christianity's age-old conflict between "idols" and the "world," and the only living God of life, has been softened. In short, man's "religion" became enhanced.

There is a great deal of truth in the opinion that our modern secularism is also to be found within the thinking of the Church. For secularism is a way of thinking that starts, not with God, but with empirical things, and on that basis builds up its philosophy of life and destiny. If Christianity is only "religion," or one "religion" among many others, what chance has it to meet the secular world? or to challenge it?

In fact, the humanism in our Christian faith has

its source only in the abandoning of the radical fact of God's revelation of himself in a real incarnation, in favor of a general "religious philosophy," which starts with man's quest for reality through a study of his environment and his intuitions. It seems utterly impossible to get beyond this type of "religion" which today is fast losing its power to appeal to sincere people. The living God alone can save us, a God who is beyond man's quest, but who meets man's quest in revelation. Outside of this we are doomed to wander around in our questing without ever hoping to find and know God.

Christianity is facing a new battle today. That battle has to do with the recovery of its inner citadel which has been largely abandoned by liberal thinkers and careless churchmen. The very science which Christian leaders were told to listen to and adjust their faith to, has now proven itself incapable of leading us onward and upward. It is a blind leader; it cannot redeem us from our hopeless and meaningless existence. These apparent friends have betrayed us. We had thought that a broadening of the Christian faith to include all religious and human quests would give Christianity a wider appeal. Instead, it has taken away even that core of high revealed Reality which we had.

We can still be scientific. But we will have to say farewell to science as a Messiah and have done with this sterile and damnable alliance with "religion" in general. We will have to become Christian again. We will need to cease using the general word "religion" to cover that which Christianity claims at its very heart, not a high human discovery but a lowly divine condescension to man from God.

Religion is man's quest, but the Christian faith is faith in God's response. Our modern Christianity is *too* "religious"; it does not claim its greatest possession. Therefore, it hesitates. Our theology is too largely "religious" philosophy and not Christian theology.

No alliance with philosophy, or science, can ever "find" this gospel of God's love. This gospel is given through revelation, and revelation is not a static presentation from God to men of a supernatural knowledge about everything. It is the sharing of God's love and purpose and hope with men who are lost in their blind and sinful egotism. No Christianity can claim the name without this vital and given fact at its core.

CHAPTER IV

SOUND THEOLOGICAL THOUGHT

PROTESTANT Churches in our country are suffering from a pernicious type of inner weakness. One might call it "theological anaemia." The very stuff which gives structure and bone to the thing we call evangelical Christianity seems to be weak. The body lacks not only red corpuscles, proper spiritual vitamines, but it lacks that calcium which can give it strength.

No Christianity can live for long without definite given facts at its very center. This does not mean that it must possess a dogmatism so intolerant that it loses its spirit of love in defending itself, and loses its sense of humility by too accurately defining God and the things of the faith. But evangelical Protestantism needs a firm structure of faith, not merely human faith, but a firm foundation of human faith in *the* Faith.

This is especially true since Protestantism inclines to become humanistic. The reformers made Christianity a matter both of the individual and of local culture. They very definitely held that Christianity was not a matter of an official Church that usurped God's sovereign Lordship and in which people who could themselves understand their faith did not count as members. The Reformers emancipated local cultures, classes, races, and the individual from an autocratic Church that had confused the means and the end.

But when Protestantism dignified the individual and the locality with such a faith and capacity, it necessarily ran the risk of individualizing and localizing the faith. In many cases individuals began to build their own faith. They made the Bible and the faith say what they interpreted it to say. In short, Protestantism humanized the Christian faith. As a result we have many denominations, and we have many opinions. Roman Catholics will tell you that this is our real problem, and that if Protestantism keeps up its atomizing tendencies, it will disintegrate itself. Protestantism can operate effectively only where its adherents are highly intelligent and responsible. The fact is that the rate of illiteracy on fundamentals is very high, even among ministers. The spirit of responsibility is waning. There seems to be nothing that holds Protestants together other than a nebulous Christian idealism. They may be held together by family relationships, old tradition, social and ethical conduct, but they are no longer bound together by faith in a common living creed. Without such unity of conviction on essential matters of the faith, it is impossible to function as a Church or as a unit of any kind. Such a Church no longer is a Church, nor can it make a common witness to the truth of God which was vouchsafed to its keeping and in obedience to which the Church can be saved. I do not care to see a return to theological bickering and hairsplitting. There is a limit to what theology can do. It is more a critical thought than a set of dogmas. But Protestantism cannot go on without a return of sound theological thinking. Mark it well! We do not need a theology so much as we need true thinking, confessional thinking.

There are things that disturb me in the modern Protestant scene. I think of the Protestant ministry in general. Many of us have lost the art of hard thinking. We no longer sit down to think through the nature of our ministry and the obligations such a task involves. We may minister to our people, we may be efficient "administers" of our churches, but there is something lacking about our preaching and our inner apologetic for being a minister of the Gospel of Jesus Christ. Our reading may be broad, but it lacks the discrimination and insight which give us authority in our realm and make our utterances relevant to the situations of life. We are not able to see the deeper things about life beyond those which magazine writers chronicle in interesting and popular fashion. We have difficulty in making the God of the gospel available and potent. We indulge in keen analysis, but we do not bring the riches of knowledge of God in Christ to bear upon that issue. We may conduct forums and discussions, hoping that thereby some solution may come, but they often turn out to be only a pooling of ignorance coupled with man's proud desire to have his say. Often our sermons are only discourses which interest ourselves and which we substantiate by a text torn out of its context to suit our whims, so that its very inner

meaning is slain by our violence to take the Kingdom
into our own hands. Or, if we be preachers whose
social zeal is beyond question, we may be so intoler-
able in our positions that we violate the very gospel
of love of which we are ministers; or social radical-
ism may so dominate our ministry as to make us
thoroughly incapable of leading people in worship
or of proclaiming the Word of God in love. Often
our social idealism lacks the corrective of realistic
insight into our gospel and the sinfulness of the
world. In short, such a ministry lacks the sound
knowledge which gives a disciplined mind. The
mind and the task are not rooted and grounded alone
in that which gives stability and structure to Christian
faith. We Protestant ministers are often not mature.
We have not learned that the mind is not meant to
be anarchistic. It is under authority. It functions
only as it serves that which is forever beyond its discovery, namely, the gospel. Using the mind as an
end in matters of Christian faith has filled the ranks
of the ministry with many who are murdering that
faith and making of Christianity a menagerie of personal notions. Until sound knowledge returns to the
ministry, Protestantism will decline. For Christianity is not a batch of personal notions. It is a definite
body of convictions based upon revelation, and the
key to its pure operation is in the ministry and the
local church.

But the ministry is not alone to blame. All along
the line, from the Church's shoddy educational work
in college and Sunday school to its capitulation in

theology to modern science, it has allowed itself to be led. One considers the Sunday-school work, good after a fashion, but highly deficient in the central issue. "Sunday-school Christianity" lacks thoroughness and preciseness, and it lacks churchly theological structure. In recent years religious educators have paid attention to individual method, but often at the expense of churchly theological content. This "Sunday-school Christianity" has "educated"(?) many away from the Church. It defeats virile church- and faith-centered worship. It has been too dilatory in introducing early adolescents and juniors to the art of worship, which is the heart of Christian life. Its concern for outcomes has caused it to overlook the in-comes of absolute realities which make for reverence and sensitive responsibility.

Theological education has offended greatly by incorporating many modern scientific and psychological studies into the curriculum without maintaining a corresponding degree of interest in theological things peculiarly conducive to the training of Christian ministers. The same is true of Christian collegiate education. Christian education in seminary or college is never natural idealism tinged with Christian sentiment. It starts always with basic axioms which are grounded in the Christian revelation.

The whole temper of modern life has been such as to enhance man and this world. Scientific achievements have created in man a sense of independence. Man's life and man's comfort were given large place. Man's emancipation from all that kept him in bondage and fear accentuated his importance in the scheme of things. His mind began to demand proof for things, and even religion was judged by its ability to give man inner satisfactions or social or economic advantages. Man decided he would not believe anything he could not accept.

It was to be expected that Protestantism, which was so closely allied with cultural life, would absorb this optimism and think of its task in terms of furthering this-worldly advances. Where churches are people's churches, in the sense that those who belong to them own them and thus temper the message of the minister, the church is apt to suffer from man's desire to control, from his uneducated whims and his unchristian cultural life, or from the minister's desire to please men. Even the hymns of such a Church exalt the human emotions, the sermons please people, the choirs entertain and its theology takes on the coloring of the human situation. The promotional activities of the Church have treated Christianity as merchandise to be advertised and sold!

The *Gestalt* psychology taught us, among other things, one very practical lesson. Persons, like movements, are *Gestalts*. They have forms peculiar to themselves. That form lies in the nature of things. A family, if it lives true to principle, in time will develop a peculiar nature. It is fed by a peculiar food; it is undergirded by a unique *Gestalt*. This is true of the Christian Church. Beneath all its outer forms it possesses an inner structural skeleton and an indigenous blood stream. It feeds on a peculiar food, it develops of itself unique and indigenous habits. At its very heart there pulsates a peculiar lifestream derived from a central source and system. Its strength depends upon its fidelity to its true nature.

My contention is that the most essential thing about the Church is being neglected in Protestant churches. I am not minimizing the adornments of the Church, in terms of art, experience, ethical habits, music, social action, theological speculation, and the like. I am concerned about the living theological structure which goes beyond and is prior to all these diversities. The Church existed before the churches. And the Church is founded upon a definite basis.

But too many extraneous things have absorbed its main task. Leaders have been drawn away from their central obligations. Cheap success in the form of earthly pomp and size has allured individuals and leaders from their bounden duties. The temper of the times has invaded the Church lacking in vigilance. The secondary effects of the Christian faith have usurped the place of primary causes. Therefore, though the Church and its leaders utter the words of the gospel, they lack force and sincere realism. The Church no longer seems real to people because its concern about God and the essential man lacks genuineness. People no longer sense the real difference between the message of the Church and that of a lecture hall, or a philosophical or ethical association. As a result, the world today assumes that the Church can be manipulated, ignored, or considered an anachronism. In some quarters it seems to be carried along by mere ancient traditions. It lives on the momentum of its past and is *used* by states, groups, parties and individuals! In fact, the Church's very structure seems to be sold out. The attempt to be a good fellow to all, to be all things to all men, has been its undoing.

No tightening of the denominational loins can solve this problem. The path ahead lies neither in fundamentalism nor in modernism. It cannot be found in the old theologies. It is to be found alone in the recovery of a living Christian theology, and that comes of sincere and creative thought, usually born of suffering.

But in many quarters theology is still ignored. In fact, many church leaders are ashamed of it. The minister's task is conceived of in terms of general ministry to men in personal, social, or oratorical ability. A prominent church leader recently said that he was amazed at the intellectual uncertainty of the ministers he visited, and that what appalled him most was the doubt many expressed as to the Lordship of Christ, and even as to the personality and existence of God! The illiterate ranter who is making a sincere witness sins less here than does the intellectual whose knowledge lacks the fundamental quality of deep understanding.

The problem is aggravated by what Dr. John R. Mott has called the serious crisis of our times. At a time when the world is falling apart because of its lack of a valid and certain and sound structure, that

very institution, the Church, which claims to speak
for God to men, is at a low ebb in positive leadership.
Instead of standing at the forefront as a prophet to
this generation, or in the midst of it as a true priest,
it halts for lack of a definite, inward apologetic.

This age does not need violent social reconstruction. It needs some sure word of the Eternal around
which its whole life may focalize. It needs integration which the true Church alone can give. What
this age needs is refuge and strength, deep healing,
and eternal stimulus. It needs a sense of the eternal
authority and meaningfulness of life in the very
midst of the anarchy of sin. No dictator can speak
that word. When Dr. Adolf Keller visited Einstein
in Princeton, that venerable scholar told him that of
all the institutions in Germany that should have
spoken a clear word to the situation none spoke save
the Church, which he, Einstein, and many others,
had thought defunct. Not the whole Church in Germany spoke, to be sure. The little remnant spoke,
and it did so, not on political or social grounds, but
on the grounds of its sound knowledge of the faith.
It witnessed to its Author out of a sense of its inner
Gestalt.

It may be that through the suffering of these days
the rapid downward trend of evangelical Protestantism will be halted. In days of liquidation we again
evaluate our real assets. The Church's present
theology is either too static and too enmeshed in an
antiquated world-outlook, or it is too fluid because
it has compromised its high theology with science and

the modern mood. We are caught between static systematic theology and mere fluid nebulous anthropology. We need living theology! We need the truth of God, less to understand it, than to confess it to the world.

The first task of the Church is to repent, and then to start at the bottom in a serious concern for the recovery not of *its own*, but *God's*, theology in Christ Jesus. The Church's refusal to see its desperate need is its sin, its ruin, and the greatest obstacle to God's revealing of Himself.

Theology is not something to be ashamed of. It is the constant and critical thought of the Church about its basis. Theology is the mental agitation of the Church in every age about its basic verities. Theological thinking is never dry nor static. It is always living and discovering. The theology of the minister must begin not with his observations of the natural world nor with his intuitions. These may enter the picture, but Christian theology always begins with exegesis in which the minister seeks to discover by critical study the objective reality that motivated those who had direct contact with the power and wisdom of God in Christ. This is the source of Christian audacity and faith.

Such thinking comes usually when the life of the Church is endangered. It restores the Church to its rightful nature and place. Such thinking is being born among us today. In its activity alone will the Church be saved, but only saved to speak to this generation about and for the God of its life.

PART II

CHAPTER V

CHRISTIAN PREACHING

TO the majority of Americans, in the larger denominations, preaching is the most characteristic thing about church life and worship. It would be difficult to think of a Sunday-morning worship service without preaching. We have been fed upon it. The popular term for the minister is "preacher." We think of Christianity in terms of preachments and exhortations. It is closely associated with evangelism.

It would not be far wrong to say that American Christianity was founded in preaching. The circuit riders were primarily preachers. Wesley's heritage is one of preaching. The frontier nursed it. Theological schools have emphasized the homiletic art. This may not be wholly true of the Protestant Episcopal Church, yet it has developed strong preachers in America, who are somewhat different from their English brethren. English Episcopal preaching is more or less dry, dogmatic, formal, and content-centered. American Episcopal preaching is doctrinal, to be sure, but it is warmly appealing, energetically intellectual, and socially passionate. The Lutheran Church, too, especially of the American type, has caught the preaching spirit.

While many people in America get their religious ideas from other than formal church sources, it is safe to say that religious ideas are disseminated largely by the pulpit. Preaching, therefore, still has a large place in American church life. Much Sunday-school teaching is really laymen's preaching. Christian teaching in a sense should be preaching.

Because it is so important it is high time that this prominent function of the Church's and the minister's office should be re-thought to determine whether it is true to its nature and purpose. I wonder just what the general impression would be if one could sit in at four or five typical American church services some Sunday morning.

Would the sermons have one thing in common? Would they confuse or integrate the person who sought to find the Christian objective about life? Would the preacher be preaching his own ideas, or would he be proclaiming a sovereign gospel to which he had seriously given assent and hearty loyalty? Would he ascend his pulpit as one who had something interesting to tell his people or would he go up into it with the feeling that he was sent to tell his people something he must tell them? Would the sermon stand out as an isolated piece of oratory on some good theme, or would it fit integrally into the whole worship as a sincere expression of God's revealed truth? Would the sermon seek merely to tell people how they ought to act morally, what they ought to think dogmatically, or would it make them conscious of an imperative from God, and cause them to do their own thinking, under a new dynamic? Would the preacher tell his people too much in the name of God, or too little? Above all, would the preacher speak what *he had heard*, or would he speak out of himself something that he had found interesting?

So we are brought to the crucial question, What is a sermon? Why is there such a thing? What is its purpose? What is preaching? The sermon is a peculiarly Protestant thing. It has always been a part of the evangelical type of Christianity. It arose out of the nature of Protestantism. Protestant leaders used it to proclaim the Word of God. By it they gave a vocal expression, or description, of the power and meaning of God in human life and history through Jesus Christ. It became an integral part of worship in the life of the Church. The Roman Catholic Church today, as in the Middle Ages, places the mass central in worship. It marks the climax of the Church's ritual and the worshipers' experience. The mass also proclaims, or dramatizes, the gospel story from its beginning in the heart of God to its end in the final consummation. The central part of it proclaims the miracles of the incarnation and the resurrection, wherein God becomes man, and triumphs in life and over death.

The sermon was meant to do what the mass did, only it was to appeal to the very core of personality through the ear. The early Reformers were afraid of idolatry, as were the prophets of Israel. Catholic worship aimed at the union of God and man, at a beatific vision of God. Protestant worship, as was true of all prophetic worship, aimed at the obedience of man to God, at man's walking with God in faithful service, in companionship with God through the means of active faith. The mass appeals too much to the eye and to the emotions. It is apt to end in idolatry or external ritualism. And it is institution or church-centered.

In Protestantism the Word of God was made supreme. It appealed to the whole man, coming through the ear to strike at the will. Protestant worship was, therefore, not aesthetic, but moral, intellectual, and spiritual. The sermon was aimed to mediate that Word of God which is like a two-edged sword, which confronts man with a decisive choice, arouses in him the sense of guilt, makes him desire forgiving grace, works like a ferment in the heart to convert men from themselves to God, binds such men together in a common fellowship of that Word, and through the power of spiritual imagination makes God a living presence and reality.

So the sermon was meant to be a high human daring, in which a man might humbly assume to address men in the name and for the sake of that living God who spoke in an act through Jesus Christ. The sermon, being living oral words, was meant to make God less a physical entity and more a personal and living power, transcendently active. In a strict sense such preaching has no method. It is sheer spontaneous *witnessing* to the power, the reality, the availability and the sufficiency of *God* in Christ in human life. Perhaps we may fittingly call it expository preaching: it discloses the living event beneath

the words of the text. It makes God the living fact
of all life.

Men preached sermons before there were preachers trained in theological schools, and before there
were written texts from which to preach. An expository sermon, then, is an attempt to witness to that
Word of God which was and is living and personal.
That Word was made human flesh and dwelt among
us. Much expository preaching is pedantic, theological, or artificial. Unless it makes the *event*
beneath the written words live, it is sterile. Preaching must always be a vital description, or disclosure
of God in contact with man.

That is what the Reformers discovered, and that
is why they exalted the sermon at the expense of
what they called an "idolatrous" mass. The mass
did not arouse men morally; it had little ethical content. Men could watch it sitting or kneeling. A
sermon makes one want to stand and sing and do.

The sermon is not merely an interesting discourse.
It is not a treatise on the relation of science to religion. It is not a "talk" on theology, sociology, or
political science. It is not based upon what the human being *desires* to hear. It is not scolding. It is
not a discussion on biblical criticism. It is not lectur-
ing, nor is it a "religious" discussion about the true
innate hungers of man for cosmic support. It is not
an argument about the existence of God, the "deity"
of Jesus, or the "sacred nature" of the Scriptures.
It is not a talk to make people give more money. It
should not be a polished statement as to why men

should be good or why they should join the church. It is not a résumé of the preacher's notions about God. It should never aim to use God for human ends. It must not even seek to make men good by telling them to be so. It should not *use* God for moral action. Never should it become a talk on psychiatry, or a discussion of the news of the week, or an essay, or an entertaining lecture.

Perhaps all of these things can be utilized in a sermon, if they are woven into it with great skill, and are subordinated to the great Subject of the sermon. But they must never usurp that Something which binds the preacher and the sermon to itself. No discourse can be called a sermon, much less can it *be* a sermon, unless it remains true to the Word of God in Christ. This is the text and the burden of every sermon. Every preacher of a sermon must know where his message begins and in what issue it shall result: humble, penitential obedience to God's revealed will and reception of his love.

Preaching, then, becomes personal address to preacher and worshiper alike, for all are responsible to the Word. It is proclamation. It is attack and invitation. It is under a great burden. The sermon is not an entity by itself; it is always an instrument. It does not deal with abstract truth as philosophy does; it deals with concrete, personal truth; with the relation of I-and-Thou in Bible fashion.

A sermon is artistry of the highest sort. The burden of the sermon is to speak of God without usurping His place. It should tell without arguing. It must not configure God to man's ideas, but do just the reverse. It must be a living dogmatism in which men are confronted with the things of the Word about which there can be no human disagreement. Preaching attacks man's disobedience to God and invites him to the life that comes through repentance and God's free love. The sermon that is based upon the Word of God will draw all hearers into the truth; it will not allow them to sit by as spectators. Preaching may be an interpretation of man's quest after God, but in a greater sense it will be a declaration of how God comes to man when man fulfills the proper requirements. Nor is all of man's questing enough. Preaching makes God in Christ so inevitable to man that nothing less, or other, than unbelief will keep him from the Kingdom.

Protestant preaching is a means. It is *a* part of worship, every phase of which is intended to do *one* thing: to make men conscious of God as their deepest problem. It is not the preacher's sermon, but a sermon of the Word, for all parts of Protestant worship are subject to the gospel's mastery. The sermon will always allow the subject to remain sovereign. To use the illustration of Lao Tse, quoted in one of Dr. Eduard Thurneysen's sermons, our words are like a wagon wheel. The wheel is useless without a hole in the center through which the axle is slipped. The wheel revolves around something that is not itself. So it is with human words in a sermon. Unless they revolve around a sovereign Subject, they remain sterile, they are mere words of man. They do not become sacrament. The strength of the sermon is not so much in the preacher as in the strong objectivity of the Subject.

The preacher dares to speak of the Subject which he is not. And he always runs the risk of making wrong, immature, or unwise statements. The best preaching will be done with a sense of failure on the preacher's part, and, in any case, God will have to use our weak and halting words to bring His Word to expression. Every great and true sermon needs the Holy Spirit to save it from being only an array of human words. For that reason the only Christian preaching that can claim the title is expository preaching.

We do not refer to that type of preaching which methodically takes as its text large passages of Scripture and comments upon them. Such preaching may be and often is dull and pedantic. Expository preaching sets forth the living Word (God in action in human flesh) or the living event beneath the words of the Scriptures. The human words are not primary. The unique thing about Christian faith is God's action. He assumes human flesh; out of an astonishing love He reconciles man to Himself. He claims lost man for Himself. He becomes man's hope, forgiveness, life, man's all, in spite of and in the light of man's lostness. Expository sermons sincerely seek to present this gospel to men. Their purpose is not to convince, but to declare the gospel sincerely and truthfully. No sermon can give birth to God or force man to believe. But a sermon can and should be so transparent that through it the living God can make Himself known *to men*. The gospel has a way of convincing men of itself.

This task of preaching is "foolishness" to the world. The preacher is a most daring man who throws bread upon the waters with firm confidence not in himself but in the power of the Word about which he preaches and which he knows in his heart can convert men.

This makes the pulpit, and the sermon, unique in Christianity. True, Buddhism and Mohammedanism have lecture stands where the law and the ritual are expounded. But no other religion has preaching pulpits from which to *proclaim* a gospel. The Christian sermon, therefore, does not speak *about* "religion," or *about* "Jesus." It proclaims realities.

Why is it that the sermon has lost this note of humility under the feeling of subjection to the great Sovereignty? Why does the Word often fail to come through the preacher's words? Where did preaching lose its note of must and ought, its awful urgency, its high appeal and attack?

For one thing, the Bible is a sadly neglected book. Modern ministers have become so absorbed with administrative duties that they too largely exclude the Bible from their concern. Further, the pew and the pulpit alike have their misgivings about the authority of the Bible. Mistakes have been found in it, variations by the thousands make the text quite uncertain, and the antedated science of the Bible makes the modern man somewhat hesitant about accepting it as a fit guide for the twentieth-century mind. The Old Testament tells of immorality, even on the part of its leaders, and the New Testament contains statements that many feel are no longer historically tenable.

Besides, there is no one view of the Bible to which Protestants hold, and consequently many take from the Bible only what *they* desire.[1] The Bible is no longer taken as the norm of faith. It is a book which men use to substantiate what *they* think. The result is that the Bible is respected, but it is "disarmed," and its message is relegated to the realm of good "moral literature," to be preserved in the long list of humanity's sacred aspirations. As a result, the Bible's Word seems to have lost its authority and uniqueness, and the modern preacher his basis for the sermon.

Of course, there are other reasons for the loss of the authoritative note in preaching. Psychology has turned the attention of people to the moods of the soul, and many follow a religion of "soul culture." New emphases are being placed upon the aesthetic and upon psychiatry. Good as they are, they have undermined that element of Christian faith which has to do with ethical obedience and the discipline of the will. Jesus is consequently made into a subjective pattern, rather than an objective Reality and gospel.

---

[1] Protestantism, by its atomism of belief and denomination, no longer presents the gospel to the world as something unitive. Man's opinions rob the gospel of its one authority.

There are many who no longer desire to hear sermons, claiming that the day of authoritative teaching is past and that the day of mutual discussion is here. The old idea of an infallible Bible, inspired in every jot and tittle, which is often associated with preaching, has run its course. People are tired of sermons which only veil a man's, or a denomination's, opinions in the name of the mighty God, and sensitive and intelligent people do not care for sermons that seek to make the Bible a textbook on science and history. Ministers are often so bewildered with their inherited wealth of scientific and historical information that they can scarcely assimilate it, much less adjust it to the permanent message at the heart of the Christian faith. This has resulted in weakening the sermon and the preaching ministry. Even the pulpit has lost its dependence upon the Bible as the sole source of Christian faith. This fact is disturbing.

Our age has grown secular. The press, the movies, fiction with its open paganism, and many other forces have reduced life to a meaningless series of thrills and superficially interesting events. Club life, saturation with interesting "talks" of every sort, the desire for something new, the drive for material happiness and comfort have made the atmosphere hostile to strong preaching. All of which is related to the emancipation of the human spirit from medieval authority. Such an emancipated spirit is quite loath to abide the authority of anyone above it. In fear of the intelligence of the worshipers, preachers dilute their message that it may appear to be intellectually respectable.

But the oustanding reason for the decline of the sermon is the change which has taken place in the minds of ministers as to the nature of the gospel. Perhaps it can be simply stated by saying that Christianity has been altered into a "human" religion, or systematic theology, whereas to the Reformers it was a realism of God and man in mutual action and response.

Christianity has become a "religion" of man instead of a revelation of the living God in action. The ethical chasm which separates man from God, and which in the Bible is called "sin," has been largely bridged by an optimistic idea of man's nature and a humanistic idea of God's nature. Man's mastery of nature has turned his head, and he will no longer admit that he is a dependent creature. Instead of looking upon Jesus Christ as the high demand of God upon him and the coming of God to man who could not redeem himself, he has made of Jesus a high comrade in man's development into divinity. Thus the whole basis of the sermon as a selfless proclamation of the good news of a God, who comes to men who are lost, is dissolved.

The old dualism between God and man has been obliterated. In the Bible, the Good News, or the "gospel," takes on the note of hilarious joy. It makes the preacher a crier of good news, a herald. His message is a *kerugma*. The message of the preacher, in the Bible, arises beyond human invention, and its source is in a sovereign act of God for man. When this distinction fades away, Christianity becomes a religion like other religions of self-culture. It no longer needs a pulpit. A religious monism needs only a Greek lecture platform, hardly an altar and a pulpit. Its high Subject no longer arises in a source prior to, and independent of, the human reflective capacities. When that becomes true, then preaching becomes only an interpretation of what is highest in man. It seeks only to mediate a rational culture. No longer do the two worlds, or wills, of God and man confront each other, for the occasion of two worlds is dissolved. The whole biblical meaning has then dropped out of sin, redemption, grace, and eternal life. The whole background of the doctrine of Christ is erased. Then preaching has lost its triumphant note, its radiant joy, its mysterious awfulness. Its life has been severed at the roots. Then sermons become essays on the religious consciousness. They deal with social problems, not with the social problem. They become analytical and negative and critical; they revert to the legalistic, the intellectual, the moralistic. They maintain the form, but deny the essence of preaching. Then sermons lose their power to produce worship, Christian conversions, and active personal faith.

The basis of the sermon is lost when the ethical dualism between God and man is easily synthesized. The whole Bible is based upon the fact of man's fall and consequent sinfulness. In the light of that fact God comes to lost men. The sermon is based upon the joyous news that He does come to men, in spite of their lostness. Thus the sermon is rooted in a basis which modern thought, by its monistic tendencies, has denied. The gospel cannot be proved, but it can be proclaimed. Christianity's central message is an assurance, a faith, a hope, a salvation, which is God's gift to man. The sermon declares that act to men.

Halford E. Luccock once said that the gospel is a great news item. Something happened to the world that could find no cause save in the marvelous love of God. God *has* saved the world. This is the fact out of which the sermon grows. Man must be told of his lostness, and, against that background, he must be told of the love of God that saves him. It is this that makes Christianity preachable and singable. The Reformers of the sixteenth century recovered the freshness of that gospel, and, as released men, they possessed a directness, a simplicity, a buoyancy that bordered on the apostolic enthusiasm. Their buoyant faith in a changing age was astounding.

It is because the sermon operates in this realm of man's sin and his salvation that the preacher has so serious and unique a task. In this realm *the* problem of life really is located, and not in the peripheral and external aspects of scientific knowledge or even philosophical ethics. The sermon has to do with man as he is facing God as He is. For this reason the sermon may become only a homily, or an inspirational "talk," instead of a proclamation of the decisive and healing word of God. A sermon based upon a mere philosophy, however cultured it may be, becomes a discussion of the preacher's opinions, which have no power to confront men with God's powerful dynamic for the redeeming of life to its high purpose in His will. When preaching degenerates to such a plane, the church in which it takes place is no longer a Christian Church, but a philosophical or ethical club, which *utilizes* the phrases of the Christian vocabulary, but which in reality is far from the essence of Christianity.

The tendency to make of Christianity a neat universal philosophy also causes sermons to lose their distinctive power. For, in a true sermon, we are concerned with One who deals with us in ways that we know to be God's ways. Christ becomes a historical center for faith; in Him we meet One who convicts us ethically as He loves us savingly. A real sermon will center in Jesus Christ, not as a moral man, but as One in whom we decisively meet and touch God. It will strike at the heart of life, which is the ego. It will always possess a radical note that draws fire and forces men to a critical decision. Every sermon is an action. It invades the world of demons which hold men in their control.

The Bible, then, is not a record of men and women whom we are to follow in morals or science, but a record of God who touched men and women in their historical situations. We are not to imitate their morals but to "catch" their God-apprehension. It is this God who meets us in Jesus Christ in all fullness. He is the text of every true sermon. For

Jesus Christ means God-in-action, in the *flesh*, for the redemption of men of faith in Him.

Sermons need not be long, because they are not the only element in Christian worship. But they should be true, and should fit naturally into the whole scheme of worship. Because the Christian faith is so closely bound up with personal relations, and these center so largely in the intimate recesses of the soul, preaching will not die out as a method of Christian propaganda and exhortation. But it will not be redeemed by oratory, or emotionalized ranting, or critical research in expensive and spacious theological seminaries. It will be redeemed only by the Word of God which is given its rightful authority in the hearts of men who dare to preach. Only the Word can save man's words from meaningless jargon. And in this case "it will not be the critic who counts, nor the man who points out how the strong man stumbles, or where the doer of deeds could have done better." In the words of the late President Theodore Roosevelt, "the credit will belong to the man who is actually in the arena; whose face is marred by sweat and dust; who strives valiantly; . . . who does know the great enthusiasm, the great devotion; who spends himself in a worthy cause. . . ." For preaching is the very aroma of living deeds, faith-in-action that proceeds from those who know by actual experience what God in Christ, with His unique power, can and will do to men.

Preaching was the highest phase of Jesus' ministry. He did not teach in the cool and methodical manner of a schoolteacher. He was an enlister. He was mastered by his Subject. Always men thought of Him in terms of decision for or against God. "He came preaching." His words were accompanied by a strange power.

Jesus never sought to give logical proof for the Subject which He proclaimed. His preaching was positive, without argument. He never adapted His subject to the *desires* of men, but only to their *understanding*. God, the Kingdom, His own consciousness, His offer of forgiveness, His Messiahship—these and many other things were never made truths capable of logical proof. They stood in their own right, and were known not through the intellect, but through obedient and repentant faith. As such His preaching was "foolishness." With Jesus, one either believes or he does not believe. In faith he is saved and in unbelief he is lost. Jesus was no "religious seeker after God"; quite the reverse. He "came" that men might have and know and see! And Jesus refused to be dragged into meaningless talk after He had spoken the truth plainly and in earnest. He was the model preacher.

Many other things undergird the true sermon. It would be misleading to presuppose that a sermon could have nothing to do with psychic and physical factors in human environment. We are bound up with our human situation. A true sermon will utilize these, but it will inject into them a strong fulcrum. That fulcrum is not man's idea of God, not man's feelings, not man's will, but the real God in

Christ. It will offer men a completely new fulcrum in life, which is God's mercy, God's grace, God's purpose, and God's Fatherhood. Rightly to preach the Christ, or the Word of God in the New Testament, is to preach with that axiom in mind as the great conviction. A sermon will not seek to establish the hearers in their own opinions of God; rather, it will seek to shatter all their opinions and give them the truth. True preaching is not when man by using Scripture passages substantiates his own ideas of God, but when man lets God be God. It seeks to make God so compelling that men must choose either for or against Him. That is preaching Christ. No other religion knows such preaching.

The sermon will not, in that case, be oratory, but the best channel for making God's reality known. It will not seek to convince people in their own mind, but to "unconvince" their minds about their own religious notions. For Christianity is not one "religion" among many others with its own peculiar God. It is Reality. "Religions" cling to that which they *think* is ultimate; Christianity declares that which is everywhere ultimate because of God who comes to man in a historical and personal event. The Christian sermon does not confront men with a "religion" higher than others; it confronts man with a choice between God's reality or man's own "religious" notions. And man's ideas of God are idols, carved out of his intuitions and interpretations, just as is the god of the ancient polytheist carved out of wood. The true preacher will seek to do what Jesus did in His

preaching: make men choose between God and anything else as God.

Truly, preaching is not a passing out to others of
the preacher's ideas. It is not confronting men with
higher standards of morals. It is not a plea for men
to turn to idealism. (Spengler once said that idealism is a coward's way out of life's tragedy. It is
the ostrich's way of avoiding danger.) What men
need is the Truth, which places them in realistic
judgment as sinners and mortals, offers them renewal
and self-respect through God's love in spite of their
sins, and endows them with a compelling will to
grasp their heavenly citizenship with a thankfulness
that issues in worshipful and meaningful action.
Sermons should not promise to give men happiness,
or more intense emotional feeling. There is something much greater than happiness—it is blessedness that comes of obedience to the will and purpose
of God. Nor should a sermon offer to make men
supermen. Rather, it should try to help them become truly human in the spirit of confession, and to
attain a grace which makes it possible for them to
live sensitively, victoriously, and fermentingly in the
midst of life as it is.

The sermon will seek to proclaim that unique
meaningfulness of life, available to all, which is
found in the living Christ of God. It will always
have as its foundation the very basis of the Christian faith, namely, that what men need is not more
knowledge but new imperatives. It will always
deny the thesis of John Dewey that more intelli-

gence will inevitably produce a better society. Rather, a greater sense of ethical responsibility born of a conviction of sin and of God's grace will make knowledge to become useful for the greater good. For that reason a sermon on science or economics is silly. The gospel deals with man's will and purpose, and not with knowledge he could discover through the intellect. It is not a question of starting where men live and raising them to higher levels of life. It is more a matter of starting with what God wills and with a realistic evaluation of man's true situation, in the hope that men may thereby be given purposeful sympathy, dynamic, and hope.

Lest anyone say that such preaching would play into the hands of the socially conservative, it might be added that it would do exactly the reverse. It would throw the authority for prophetic utterances back upon the sovereign Word of God, and not upon the mere changing opinions of the preacher. It would redeem the pulpit from its discredit because it tries to be an authority in alien fields, by giving it a place and a task unique unto itself. There is enough social dynamite in the preaching of such expository sermons to blast human pride and make way for a greater eternal meaningfulness and brotherly comradeship in life. It would save the monastic from a seclusion apart from his brethren who belong to him organically, and it would save the materialistic Communist and racial Fascist from the vicious collectivism that denies the transcendence of reality and refuses men freedom to choose for

God. Such preaching would strike at the deepest problem of society and would save us from the fragmentary and superficial attempts that are now being made to establish a new truly human society. Sermons must invade the demon world with the only power that can drive demons out.

This basic preaching, if it remained biblical, would correct some of the deplorable spiritual illiteracy of the churches. It would restore a much-needed "sound knowledge." For all phases of life are dealt with in the Bible. Besides, the realistic way of thinking in moral terms, which is peculiar to the Bible, would begin to filter into community life. The preacher would be saved from himself and from the difficulty of seeking suitable texts. His work would become simpler and more effective. He would not be at the mercy of man's mental desires. Further, such preaching would unite men's minds in a common truth that would rescue us from the terrible divisiveness that now scatters our church and community unity. The preacher would be helped to escape from an apologetic preaching that results only in an uneasy temporary settlement of the mind, when what Christianity proposes is a decisive loyalty of the heart with infinite resources at hand to bring the sure kingdom of God to fruition.

CHAPTER VI

THE NEWER BIBLE

A GREAT deal of the Christianity in the United States could be called "Bible Christianity." We are Bible people. Most of our denominations are founded on a strictly biblical basis. By that we mean that they slight the whole history and tradition of the Church and go back to the New Testament as the only basis of Christian faith. The sectarian idea, which holds that a church is after all a voluntary society of Christians who are banded together like the early Church, is strong among us. Hence, democracy in church life is our ideal. We enhance the individual at the expense of the Church.

In derision, a vast section of the United States is loosely termed "the Bible belt." In this "belt" the Bible is still highly regarded, though not so much as the mediator of the Word of God as an infallible book of moral laws and religious regulations. The Bible is like a fetish, and its legal precepts are minutely observed and defended, but the Church plays a minor rôle, since the individual Christian is the primary consideration. The Church is only an after-thought. In that respect typical American Christianity is like the government of our country. The State, as such, is only an after-thought, while the individual is the primary consideration. We have Bible conferences, Bible institutes, Bible training schools, and Bible colleges. In a sense much of our preaching is still biblical.

Notwithstanding this high regard for the Bible, we use it with little understanding as to its nature. We have not really discovered *the* Bible in the Bible. Critical knowledge of the Bible has only slowly filtered into our popular church life. Most people fear even the mention of it, lest it upset their pet notions as to the literal infallibility of the Book. The Bible is, therefore, still the source of our divisions. We make it say many things. We use it as a quarry from which to mine ore to mold our pet notions, and as a source book for the support of our systems of thought and our rules of action. We try to make it substantiate democracy, Prohibition, antiwar resolutions, Socialism, and everything else that might seem good. We read the Bible casually, hoping to get its meaning by a perusal of its surface.

Is this right? Is this the Bible's real message and concern? Is the Bible a moral lawbook good for today? Can its morals be practical today? Is it a sourcebook for our church practices and governments? Does the Bible even primarily substantiate democracy and Prohibition and Socialism and capitalism? Is the Bible a supernatural fetish, infallible in every dot and period and comma? Is it right to use the Bible in such a way as to make it substantiate our church divisions? Does the Bible even claim to be a divine book, like the Book of Mormon?

It is difficult to find the true meaning of the Bible without some knowledge of the critical scholarship of the last one hundred years. While in many respects that scholarship has been destructive, in a much larger sense it has liberated us from all these untenable notions of an infallible book, and has revealed to us a Bible within the human Bible that is even more potent and contemporary than our daily newspapers.

The Bible has always been a unique book. Its preservation and its vitality are matters for wonder and study. While the Church, either Jewish or Christian, was in existence before the books of the Old or New Testaments were collected into an authentic canon—or before most of them were even written—nevertheless, the Bible of the Old and New Testaments has been the basic source and resource of the Christian faith.

The Protestant Reformers of the sixteenth century denied to the Church the primary authority. They found, through personal experience initiated by a reading of the Bible, that no pompous external institution had a right to usurp sovereign, divine truth. Their Christian experience was traced directly to God, who saved men by a direct method through grace and the Holy Spirit, mediated through the Bible. The Word of God, said the Reformers, was first, although the Word and the Church are inseparable. They complemented each other, but the Church must be a Church of the Word.

It has been said that Protestantism, therefore, set up the "paper pope" of an infallible book to replace the human pope. True, Protestantism has been in a sense the Christianity of a book. But far more, Protestantism has been the Christianity of the Word of God which the Reformers said confronted all men who read the Bible in an humble spirit through the aid of the Holy Spirit. The human Church, as well as the Bible, is only a necessary effect of the Word of God.

As a result, the Word of God became central in Protestant worship and work. The sermon was based upon it. Ministers were trained in its exposition, and the ministry derived its function from the Word. The Church, and theology, were bound to the Word. It was made available to all men through many translations. The common vernacular of modern languages took on biblical terms.

Early Protestantism held to a paradoxical conception of the Bible as the Word of God. Luther could say that the Scriptures alone are the Word of God, and, yet, that the Word of God was "cradled" in the Scriptures. Luther did not always identify the Word of God with the words of the Bible. And he busied himself with biblical criticism, which indicated that he was not a slave to the letter, but a seeker of the right words and their proper meanings so that the human words might yield up their original divine thought and intention.

The Reformers lived very close to the medieval idea of the Bible, as an infallible and mysterious book of divine information. It was to be expected, therefore, that they would sometimes seem to slip back into the crudest literalism. Luther appealed to a verse of Scripture in its literal form in his debate with Zwingli. (Of course, the debate involved more than the text he appealed to, for Luther suspected Zwingli's humanistic interpretation of all Christian themes under discussion.) Calvin sometimes falls into the same literalism. But both were forced by their own personal experience to regard the Bible as something to be studied with critical care. And both were forced to make a distinction between the words of the Bible and the living Word which it mediated through the power of the Holy Spirit and faith. Both felt that only the Spirit of God could make the words of the Bible yield up its secret Word. Both saw that the Bible was not a divine lawbook, sacredly infallible in every detail, but a personal address to men from God.

The Word of God is the important message and the power of God to and in man. It is only in the Bible that we may learn of God's mercy and judgment. Therefore, the Word of God is vitally linked up with the human words of the Bible. Thus Protestantism began the process of freeing the Bible from its literalism, and, while preserving its human makeup as important, made the significant discovery that God's Word and personal relation with men lie beyond literalism and bibliolatry. The human Bible only introduces us to God as personal historical Saviour. For deeper than history, deeper than human words, deeper than the human Bible is the God who is beyond trifling discrepancies and verbal inaccuracies.

In some quarters of Protestantism a rigid dogmatism later developed the theory of a plenary inspiration of the Bible, which made of it an almost magical creation, accurate in all its details, whether historical, scientific, or social. In a former day such a theory held charm for people who longed for some external security and authority. In truth, these people made the Bible a material pope. They made it a rigid book of divine laws and proof texts instead of a living book of God's life and love.

Few intelligent Protestants can still hold to the idea that the Bible is an infallible book; that it contains no linguistic errors, no historical discrepancies, no antiquated scientific assumptions, not even bad ethical standards. Historical investigation and literary criticism have taken the magic out of the Bible and have made it a composite human book, written by many hands in different ages. The existence of thousands of variations of texts makes it impossible to hold the doctrine of a book verbally infallible. Some might still claim for the "original copies" of the Bible an infallible character, but this view only begs the question and makes such Christian apologetics more ridiculous in the eyes of sincere men.

Critics in the last century, and even before, began their onslaught upon the Old Testament. Science had its difficulties with the story of creation, with biblical cosmology, and with the Flood. Historians had their difficulties with the records and the chronology of the Bible. Almost everyone had diffi-

culties with the miracle stories of the Old Testament, and many were repelled by the immorality of
some biblical heroes. But the historical and scientific discrepancies in the Bible were not all that
robbed the Bible of its unique nature. There were
other forces at work.

On the basis of the evolutionary theory, scholars
began to explain the origin of the Hebrew religion
by various steps and by certain progressive acquisi-
tions of religious ideas from other nations. We
began to speak of the "religious literature" of the
Hebrews. The religion of the Bible was studied in
the light of the history of general religious ideas.
Courses formerly unheard of were catalogued in college and seminary curricula, such as the literature of
the Bible, the religion of the Hebrews, the problem
of the Mosaic authorship of the Pentateuch, the rise
of Hebrew religious ideas after the exile, and the
like. In time, such courses were developed in con-
nection with New-Testament study.

What happened was that the Hebrew-Christian
sacred writings were made similar to other religious
writings, and the Hebrew Christian tradition lost
its radical nature. The Bible took its place with
other religious literature, and even the Church in
some sections began to desert the Bible as the only
spring of its life. The idea of the Word of God
mediated through the Bible was given up, and in
its stead the Bible was regarded by literalists as an
infallible collection of proof-texts for dogmatic
theology, and by liberals as one of the collections of

religious literatures among the many already in existence, not unlike others. The paradoxical nature of
the Bible as held by the reformers was abandoned.

There are admirable and helpful books which do
not escape the modernistic idea that the Bible, in
spite of its many discrepancies and peculiarities, must
be interpreted in the light of the age in which it was
written; that it enunciates only truths of *general
wisdom* and "religion," like those in any other religion, except that they may be more refined and
synthetic. The "abiding" value of the Bible must
be sought beneath the "changing" forms. True, but
what *is* abiding? High *human discovery* of "religion" of *the* only revelation of God?

Thus we today face a dilemma. On the one hand
liberals have made of the Bible a book of general
"religious literature," to be placed in the pantheon
with that of other religions. As such the Bible has
lost its unique place. On the other hand the Bible
has become a sort of infallible fetish, miraculously
inspired by God, without error or fault. Thus the
Bible itself is practically worshiped. But such an
idea is unrealistic.

Both ideas are a liability, yet both contain great
truths. The Bible does have aspects of general religious literature, but it has a unique story to relate.
It is a question whether this inner story belongs to
general religious literature at all. Its message, seen
in modern light, confronts us as unique. The Bible,
with its mysterious and unique nature and content,
has been preserved at great odds throughout the

centuries. It is the only place where the story of the beginnings and roots of the Christian faith is preserved. It is, indeed, the Book of books.

The greatest ages of Christian power have been those in which the Bible was read, and when it spoke to men of God. Today, wherever the Christian Church is facing real enemies in a deadly struggle, as in Germany, the Bible is being read with new understanding. It is being read in a far different way from that of the fundamentalist or the modernist. It is not being read for its history, or its sociology, its science, its ethics, or its literature. The Bible confronts confused men today with something far more than these, and with a reality that transcends all "religious" ideas of other religions.

What we face in the Bible is not man's invention but God's revelation. The Bible does not seem to be interested in literature as such. True, the form and beauty of its literature is evident, but that is not the main thing about the Bible. Many might dispute the literary quality of the common, or *koine*, Greek, in which the New Testament was originally written. It is the *content* of the Bible that makes the literary form what it is. The real nature of what the Bible seeks to say is beyond the form of human literature; it tells about something which no other literature contains. The Bible is not primarily a literature. It is witness about God.

The Bible contains much history, some of it faintly embedded in age-old myths, folk tales, battle songs, campfire recitals, and the like. But, in the realm of history, the Bible is far from satisfying to the accurate historical scholar. History in the Bible seems suspended. It is difficult to account for the actions of the men and women of the Bible on historical grounds. Abraham goes out not knowing whither he goes; Moses responds to a call from beyond history and pursues a course that no one, who lives by the ordinary standards of selfish life, would pursue. Prophets come forth under the impulse of a mandate from somewhere beyond the realm of time. A nation is born for a cause and a purpose quite unlike any other nation. And One appears who goes His strange way upon the earth to a cross—and for what historical reason? None! But God! And God is anything but natural history. There is interesting history in the Bible, but the Bible is not primarily interested in telling accurate historical stories. Its history lacks chronological continuity and scrupulous scientific accuracy.

But, surely, the Bible teaches morality? Yes, and no. Side by side with the loftiest moral codes the world has ever seen we have the unholy stories of Abraham attempting to sacrifice his son, Jacob deceiving his blind father, Solomon with his many wives, Elijah slaying the priests of Baal. In spite of its dignified moral teachings, the Bible is not primarily interested in morality. In any case, morality seems to be only a by-product of something else. We cannot follow all the morality of the Bible today.

Surprising as it may seem, the Bible is not interested in "religion." The Bible says very little about how we may be "religious." It dwells not on those different reactions which men have, and make, to that mysterious, natural world without or within the soul. Other religions surpass the Bible in their concern for the *human* approach to God. The Bible is remarkably devoid of mysticism, which seeks to find God in the mystic subconscious realm within the soul. It has little to say about the ethically active people who hope to arrive at the throne of God by their sincere good works. If it mentions them, it is to deprecate and condemn them. And the Bible has little to say about the intellectual dogmatists who make their way the only one into the realm of God. In fact, the Bible does not antagonize the unreligious publican so much as it attacks the "religious" man. Even when the rituals of the Temple and the sacrifice are offered to Israel, it is always with the understanding that something more is required of man than mere religious ceremonies. Little is made of "religious experience" in the Bible as an *end* to be sought in itself.

The Bible is hardly a collection of biographies of religious men, for it neglects to give us the very things about the life of a hero which will enable us to understand him. Biographies have been written about the "life" of Jesus, yet the Gospels are not biographies. They give us so little of what we deem necessary in order to understand Jesus Christ.

Even the Church, whether in the New or the Old Testament, is not a perfect Church. We often hope to restore the New-Testament Church, yet many respectable churchmen would not care to associate with some of the Christians who formed the first congregation in Corinth! We of this age should scarcely desire to worship with those "spiritual gypsies" gathering in homes, without order, or minister, or the surroundings of Gothic architecture, for the true Church of the Bible is little more than a portable chapel. Its reality is beyond fallible human beings gathered together. From the human and religious point of view, there is nothing pretentious about either the lowly Jesus of Nazareth or His Church!

The people of the Bible are realists. They do not make their "religion" what we so often make ours, namely, something that takes us out of our human situation and puts us into a divine company of perfect people; out of the sinner class into the sinless class. Bible people are utterly human.

The people of the Bible are not spectators; they are participants. They do not play rôles; they live life. The Bible tells about man as he is within, face to face with his elemental humanity. Biblical people do not make escapes from life by dividing life between the sacred and the secular. To them man is a unit. The righteous man is not the *sacred*, or divinized, man, but the God-apprehended man. And the true Church does not usurp the power and the authority of God's lordship over men. The true Church, and the truly righteous men in the Bible are humble servants. The blazing indignation of Jesus and the prophets is "antireligious." It punctures the pride of the religious man.   It exalts the sinner and the publican.

There is a distinction about the thinking of the Bible.   There is little speculation in it.   All its thought is realistic, concrete, ethical, and forthright. There is no sophistry; there is no metaphysical argument.   The thinking of the Bible is done under the authority of God.   Life is considered as a confrontation of two realities—God and man.   And man is not regarded as an individual but as a part of the social group.   Thought is always dominated with a sense that life is under a transcendent mission.   And the premise of Bible-thinking is not that man is the measure of all things, but that God is that measure, and that the ethical, not the intellectual, is life's most important problem.

Bible-thinking is not direct; that is, it does not seek to explain things exhaustively, as did Greek thinking.   On the contrary, it was a type of "broken thinking," in which men lived a life of faith without logical explanations.   Thus Bible-thought was not concerned with nature, or with the unity of the world in itself.   Bible-thought is always dominated by a future hope, not by an age of glory already past. Bible-thought is therefore optimistic, because it is premised upon God.   Bible-thinking is God-thinking, it is heart-thinking coupled with a strong ethical note.   It thinks about God and life as a hungry man thinks about food.   It is thought always under necessity.   There is no thinking like it anywhere else in the world.   It is a type of thought unique in the discovery of the real meaningfulness of life and the reality of God.

Biblical people are not "finders" of God. Rather, they act and speak as though they *had been found* and called of God. They never claim to know God of themselves. They know God because He has made Himself known to them. They are not people who live by their own security. They have abandoned their own security and rest upon the security of God. They live lives of faith in God. God is not a human projection to themselves. They live by God's revelation, or God's sharing His life with them. They never reach God by high thinking, or by deep meditation, or by the effort of doing good works. God is not an object of *their* mind. He is always Himself, and addresses man as apart from man. God exists, even apart from man. Bible people's lives are derived from God. They are not identified with omnipotent matter, with an All-soul, or an abstract Being, of some kind. To them God is concrete and sovereign God, and man is man when he lives in faith in God.

It is this God who seeks and comes to man in Christ Jesus. Jesus is the Word of God, and as such He reveals the secret of God. Jesus is not an intensified Man, nor even the bringer of man's highest ideas. He is the One through whom there comes something new, something which the world cannot of itself create. He cannot be proven, or even analyzed. He stands in His own right as ONE WHO IS WHO HE IS! He is to be believed and followed or rejected and neglected. In that respect He is the very core of the biblical message, and the coming to light of that which the Old Testament constantly seeks to disclose and to which it points. The Bible never labors in the field of seeking for God; it always witnesses to the God who *has* revealed and *is* revealing Himself.

The revelation of God consists not in mighty displays of eternal power. The Bible speaks directly and simply and without fanciful tales of the creation by God. It is not interested in the scientific side of creation, nor in the mythological elements in the Genesis story, but in the fact of God's creative sovereignty. Even myths can reveal God's Word. It is not interested in the psychology of evil, but in the mysterious *fact* and the *way* and the *consequence* of evil in man's disobedience and prodigality. It is not interested in scientific explanations of the burning bush, nor in the psychological genesis of the call of Moses. It is interested in stating it as a fact of God's sovereign way with man.

From beginning to end, the unifying and meaningful fact of the Bible's varied literature, history, poetry, morality, and religion is the fact of God. He is witnessed to and never explained. The Bible is not a textbook for the betterment of humanity, but a witness declaring the decisive beginning and activity of God in human lives and in human history. The sovereignty of God is the Bible's one message. There is no other cause for the unhistorical actions of biblical people than that they were apprehended of God and obeyed Him. There is no other way by which one can obtain any real unity in the whole Bible record.

It is perfectly evident that this revelation of God actually took place in human history. The Bible is only a series of *human* records seeking to tell about what God did in the lives of men and women who took Him at His Word and lived in obedience to His sovereign leading. The Word of God is greater than the words of the Bible, for it is primarily an act of God, an event of God in human flesh. This Word of God holds the words of the Bible together. The Word of God is the living Truth of the living God, which becomes contemporary in any and every age and heart where men sense His Lordship through the medium of the historical revelation.

It is this directness, this newness, that strikes us on reading the Bible. In this respect, it is different in *kind* from other religious literatures. True, there is "religious" material in the Bible. But always the God of the Bible seems to war against mere human "religiousness," which becomes a substitute for God's Lordship. General religious morality may be defined as the effort of a person who seeks to improve himself by high ethical culture. The morality of the Bible is a quality of responsible living that results from what God means to life. Religious morality, or ethical theism, may be man's highest possible achievement, but biblical morality is that which results when man ceases to be moral and acts upon God's direct mandate.

There is something awfully drastic about the
Bible, in that it proclaims the beginning of God at
the very surrender of man at his best. It addresses
man; it does not argue. Nor does it invite criticism
of its Subject. This conception of God as truly great,
as the One who is first and last, as the Lord of life
and death, as the One we can wholly trust, as the
One who will not be satisfied with anything less
than the primary and whole devotion of man, is
decidedly biblical.

Jesus, whom we have diluted to a very gracious
lover of men, was no less drastic in His demands
upon men. When we confront Him, we are always
aware of God. God was Jesus' primary concern.
He is God incarnate. The rich young ruler confronted the same God-reality, as did Saul of Tarsus.
The words concerning publicans and harlots going
into the Kingdom before the "religious" leaders only
indicate that the possessive and acquisitive qualities
of men (not only regarding monetary wealth, but
moral and intellectual wealth), make men gods unto
themselves, who treat the real God as a mere annex
to human life. This renders it quite impossible for
them to make the great necessary surrender of the
inmost life to the Kingdom ideal. And only in the
insight that God is Lord can one see the Kingdom.
All of Jesus' words are based upon that premise.

This is *the* Bible. The Bible is the record of the
reality that broke forth upon the earth, gripping and
arresting men and women independent of, and at the
expense of, their "religious" qualities or aptitudes.

The Bible witnesses to that event in history which we associate with God in Israel and with Jesus of Nazareth, from whom and in whom and because of whom a new power and force and mentality issued, which cannot be explained on the basis of history or morality or science or even "religion." The Bible speaks a stark God-realism. The biblical God is not a God of natural or historical or psychological process. He is the uncaused and unconditioned. He, whom men dimly surmise, revealed Himself.

Out of the last extremity of life itself, even death, this God speaks; not so much by human words as by divine meaningfulness and dramatic action, lest it be materialized or rationalized by man the inveterate idolater. Out of the very birth of man, even in a cradle, God breaks forth with a new meaningfulness for all human life. Between these two mysteries, life and death, this Day of man, the whole realm of man is encompassed. In this human flesh of ours the living God comes to men declaring Himself sovereign in judgment and mercy. He is Lord of life and death. This is the message of the Bible, and all else is but a derivation of this mighty revelation.

Thus the Bible is not a textbook on "religion" or the "philosophy of religion." Nature and man are not primarily exalted. God is revealed and man and nature are derived. The glory of nature in the Bible is that it is God-derived! It has no divinity of its own. And in the consciousness that they are derived, Bible men become strong. It is the living witness of a deed—yes, *the* deed—of God for and in men. And we still live in the *same* stream of human history in which this deed took place. To *us* a Child *is* born, to *us* the resurrection *is* given. The human words of the Bible may be weak, and even incapable of adequately witnessing to what God is and does, but the Word of God does come through them, and through them alone.

For any who try to understand the Bible and its events as sheer history or science there is nothing but disappointment. The Bible takes for granted man's longing for a cosmic home, his desire for eternal sanctions for his actions and his need for an inspiration beyond himself to lend meaningfulness to his life. It deals with the answer to the great and ultimate question of human existence, its why, its whence, its how. It focalizes in man's will-to-believe in something beyond himself, but more in God's miraculous condescension to meet man in his bewildering lostness, of which man is often not clearly conscious. The Bible records the story of God's grace.

The Bible is a Jewish book. Even the New Testament is a Jewish book. And it is no exaggeration to say that "salvation is of the Jews," for from them has come that unique and necessary way of salvation for the total man. No writings that merit the standard of the biblical canon have come from Gentiles. True, the Gentiles were not prepared for such a task, but it is truer that the Gentile mind and language did not have the genius to receive God's revelation. The Hebrew language is a religious language. It is poetic without being sentimental. It is not artificial, nor does it have that cultural frill which makes religion a mere human interest.

Since this is so, the Bible is bound to take on a more vital character than ever before. It will not be subordinated to the Church in the Catholic sense, although the Church did exist before the canon of the New Testament was formed, or before some of its books were written. It will not be a magically infallible book of divine truth, recorded by human robots, which provides every denominational church with a basis for its existence on the basis of proof-texts. Nor will it be the "religious literature" of a particular people of the ancient world, to be synthetically understood in the light of all other sacred writings.

We have outgrown all these phases of biblical understanding. There are certain truths in all of them. But we will need to look in a different direction for the authority of the Bible. The Bible must be seen, not in what it is in *itself* but in *what* it confronts man with, and in what it says to men who give themselves wholeheartedly to what it seeks to declare. That is nothing less than God, God in action, God in life, not in terms of what man constructs out of *his* religious consciousness, but in terms of what God shares, with what He thinks about man, and with what He can do for and with man. That is the Word of God, which, while paradoxically united with the words of the Bible, is nevertheless beyond the human words and is not necessarily bound by them. The Bible is not the actual Word of God, but merely a human witness to what the Word of God did in and with men and history.

The words of the Bible are not to be believed because they are in the Bible. The Scriptures are true to me because God by His Holy Spirit tells me they are true. I do not worship the Bible blindly. Nor do I hear God's word in the Bible because *I* feel that I do. But in reading the Bible there comes to me a strange language, there confronts me a real God, and there emerges before me something about life that I do not discover anywhere else. It reaches me, it grips me, it offers me a new way and a new anchorage of life. It is because the Scriptures do this that they are "sacred."

Not all of the Bible does this for me. There is much in the Bible that is like chaff, or, rather, like some of the seemingly insignificant parts of a watch. I must *"search"* the Scriptures to get its central meaning. Its message is not on the surface. Yet the message of the Bible comes through to those who read with the right spirit. There is a residue in the Bible that remains intact in spite of all its inaccuracies, its antedated cosmology and science. The real struggle today is not between the Bible and science but between the biblical viewpoints upon man and God, and unbelief.

In recent years much has been made of the doctrine of progressive revelation. By this we interpret the "religious" history of the religion of Israel and the religious history of the early Church on the basis of the theory of evolution and social psychology.

True, we must grant that much in the religious development of Old-Testament religion is better understood when we know that many ideas and folk-tales in that period were assimilated from neighboring tribes and nations. True, there seems to be a growing idea of God from the days of the Hebrew tribal society through its days of nationhood to the post-exile period. There is also much truth in the idea that the New Testament reveals a development in religious ideas, from the days of Jewish Christianity to those of the universal Gospel of John.

But there is a unity throughout the Bible, in spite of evolutionary development. The God of the Bible has certain qualities different from those of all other gods. There is in the Bible a note of the unity of God, the unity of His purpose in prophecy, the righteousness of God, the personality and mercy of God. And it lacks all the fantastic notions often associated with religious deities, as well as the mystical and intellectual esotericism. In short, *revelation* and *God* do not progress. The unity of the Bible is not in its developing human "religious ideas," but in the progressive understanding of the *one true God who was* revealing Himself to Abram as to John.

The idea of progressive revelation may help us to understand the human side of the revelation process, but it does not account for the fact of the constant reality of the divine revelation. For this biblical revelation is a unit which cannot be assimilated into the idea of general religious revelation, because it possesses a quality unlike general religions. Jesus

Christ does not come at the end of an evolutionary revelation of "religion"; He is the fullness of that which was being revealed, but dimly apprehended, in the Old Testament. Our modern incandescent bulbs are made for the same electricity that aroused the curiosity of Benjamin Franklin. There is no evolution in electricity. Thus the revelation-reality of the Bible is a unit.

It is, therefore, easy to see why the Bible never makes any claim to being in itself sacred. The Bible, like the people it describes, does not purpose to isolate itself from all that is human. Its power and authority rest neither in its human inaccuracy, nor in its "religious" superiority. It is only a servant to the Word. That is why the Bible says more between and beyond the lines than it says in the words. Those who come to it as though it were a magic book whose secret lies in just the reading of it will be disappointed. The Bible does not yield its secret by magic. The Bible is not a "religious" book which must be kept under guard, or on a sacred pedestal, to be read by the select. Nor does it need human defense. The Word is its secret, and it will yield that secret to those who approach it with humility and teachableness.

Similarly, the secret of Jesus' nature is never revealed to those who approach Him in a proud, critical or historical attitude. The secret of Jesus is seen not by "flesh and blood," but by those who can see beyond His frail humanity; who can hear beyond His physical words (Jesus never spoke many words, and for a reason), and who can discern His inner reality by a quality of life best described as reverent, humble, and obedient. Only the humble, the repentant, and the obedient know who He is. So it is with the Bible. It says little about the physical side of men's lives. It presents an array of frail and sinful men. But to the discerning, there is discoverable at work in and upon them, something beyond time and space and history.

The Bible, it can be said, is coming back into its own. The modern crisis of life is forcing us back upon essential things which are always true because they are elemental, and, in a sense, primitive. For man, in spite of his modernity, is a simplicity. In this respect the Bible's "science" of life transcends the centuries, for its Subject does not change and decay as does history. Further, the biblical criticism which shrouded the Bible in a haze of uncertainty and made it an unknown and anachronistic book—in spite of being a "best seller"—is becoming more humble. The Bible's simple message is beginning to break through our speculations. It is one thing to "explain" biblical ideas and their evolutionary development; it is quite another thing to discover the secret of the power of men who affirmed life with divine meaningfulness in other days of crises similar to our own.

It is to be hoped that a frank rereading of the Bible, with modern glasses, will make it again a meeting place for all Christians, who will find in it the very source of all life that calls itself Christian.

What care we whether *our* ideas of the Bible agree or not. That is not the important thing. Faith in the Bible's God is needed, not "religious" ideas. For it is true that our "religions" will get us nowhere. They will only divide us the more and mire us deeper into our own subjectivism. The Bible bids us desist from religious quests and around it meet the God who is God, who does not support any religious quester or denominational proof-texter. The Bible tells of a God who will be the first and the last, the Judge and Saviour Himself. He has not resigned His sovereign right into the keeping and defense of any human being, theologian, school, or denominational group.

Unless this becomes true among us the Christian "religionists" will kill the Christian faith, or will make it, in the eyes of the world, something that it is not. They will rend the Bible asunder to satisfy the demands of their own humanistic ideas. Then the God they worship is no longer God, but *a* god created not out of wood or stone, but out of man's ideas.

The Bible is not itself *the* answer to man's quest, but it *points* to the answer. Therefore, the Bible is not a book to be read now and then, as Dr. Visser 't Hooft says, but a book to be struggled with until it blesses us, until its God speaks to us.

CHAPTER VII

RECOVERING THE CHURCH

WE need to remember that the Church is something divine to which, in a sense, *men come*, and not something human which goes after men in an undignified manner. The voluntary financial support of our churches has contributed to a conception of the Church as a human institution that depends upon human efforts for its existence. The same is true of our evangelism and of our many activities within the churches to make them "going" concerns.

The lack of order and dignity within American churches is due to the same cause. Ministers too seldom think of their function as in any way peculiar and sacred. Worship suffers likewise. Religious education within the churches is more concerned with the development of experience in the individual than with the glories and the importance of the Church. We often make people feel that the Church needs them, but we neglect the Catholic emphasis that they need the Church. In fact, our individualism has been anti-institutional. We have been afraid of external uniformity lest it jeopardize individual freedom.

Much of our thinking needs correction at this point. We need a new conception of and a new emphasis upon *the Church*. Only so will the churches in America be able to confront their social situation with a common witness to the Word of God entrusted to, and *only to,* the Church. And only in unity of this deeper sort will there be any strength.

This confusion as to what "Church" means must be cleared up by serious thinking. It is a common thing to hear people criticize the Church for this or that, or to have men say that the Church should do this or that. The Church is surely not the ministry, nor the people in the churches, nor the building, nor the officials of the churches. There is another element involved in the nature of the Church, which lies beyond all these, and which must be recovered in the American churches.

We American Christians do not have an adequate conception of the Church. Most of us think of the churches. Because of our peculiar church history, which has never known *one* Christian Church, we lack what the Europeans have in their idea of the holy Catholic Church. To us the Church is a group of religious people and not a divine idea which exists in the mind of God whether there are men or not. Too much of our Christianity ends with the individual's conversion and sanctification. This is unfortunate, and one great reason for our lack of a corporate sense of *Church* unity. Further, we are far removed from the ruins of Christian churches, and from the great cathedrals of Europe which give men a sense of belonging to something venerable, ongoing, and historic. And because our history began in a revolutionary attitude toward everything of the Old

World and was fed by a stream of immigration largely bent on escaping the old church forms of aristocratic Europe, we lack the historic background and perspective whereby we might have high regard for the traditions of the Church.

Besides, our pragmatic attitude is of such a nature that we grow impatient with ideas, with anything that does not have direct usefulness. The churches, when caught in this temper, were bound to think of themselves as personally or socially useful. For that reason our churches have not developed a strong theology of the Church. Our churches are sectarian types, and, as such, are divisive and exclusive, not unitive and inclusive. They have regarded their peculiar beliefs and practices as far more important than the great unitive doctrines of belief held by the historic Church. Their anti-State-Church and anti-Roman attitudes have made them cautiously guard themselves against any encroachments of a "Romanizing" character. Even the architecture of American churches betrays a lack of catholicity.

Many people do not like the word "church." It sounds cold and institutional. It reminds them of a building, constructed of stone, brick, or wood. It represents a formal organization, based upon a theological creed, which one joins, or a denominational structure with its attendant officialism. It lacks warmth and personality. It seems distant from the average person's realm of life and daily pursuits.

The Church is an especial problem in these days. It is the expression of Christianity which is most evident to the average man, who may not know much about either the Bible or Christian theology. The Church is the point at which Christianity becomes incarnate and practical. Therefore it is highly important that Christians concern themselves with the nature, the function, and the basic justification for the Church in this world.

Today, when men are realistically evaluating all the inherited institutions to ascertain whether they have a reason for being, the Church must stand the test of realistic examination. The external Church often becomes a substitute for the Church of the Word. And when that happens the form has usurped the essence, the means has become the end. In such cases institutions either die, or they readapt themselves by a revitalization of their true nature and function. The crisis of the modern Church involves just such a revitalization from within if it would have a solid foundation beneath it. The true Church of Jesus Christ is neither denominational nor organizational, but an organism of human beings, who know they are sinners and who cohere in common responsible obedience to the living reality which Jesus Christ is, namely, to the Word of God.

Before there was a Christian Church, there was a Church, which consisted of people who lived in faith in God. That faith centered in the promise of a coming Messiah; it did not center in man's quest for God, but in God's promise, which is God's grace. The minds of these people were turned toward the promised Christ. This hope was in reality a faith in Christ, and Christ was God's love, God's act of sharing Himself with sinful men.

Jesus had no thought of establishing an organized Christian Church. He always thought of Himself as an integral part of the Church of His day. True, the Church of His day was far from being the true Church. It was filled with ecclesiasticism, officialism, pharisaism, legalism—in short, humanism. It had largely lost its spirit of service and had become a proud, cold, self-sufficient organization, with established codes of conduct and belief. It was hardly Church, though there were many of His day who saw what the Church had become and hoped for its restoration. But Jesus had no idea of establishing another institution to compete with the Church of His day.

Yet He regarded Himself as coming at the end of a process in revelation. No one can escape that note of decisiveness and finality in Jesus' own mind. In the light of what He was and what He said, the pre-Christian Church should have repented, adapted itself repentantly to the new truth, and entered into a new realm of life. Jesus did gather to Himself a group of disciples, but He hardly thought of them as elders in a new Church. Rather, they were to be His disciples who would furnish new cells for the old institution.

After His earthly career early Christians never thought of themselves as separated from the historic Church. They incorporated Jesus and His revelation into their previous customs and thought.

When the old refused to adapt itself to the ferment of the new, there was great tension. Paul had hoped that no rupture would result between the Christian fellowship and Judaism. But it came. The Christian fellowship then launched out upon its own career, although it did not give up the old.

It is unfortunate that the Christian fellowship soon forgot its former connections, and in time became so self-conscious as to forget its Judaistic home. It is to the shame of the Christian fellowship that in time it grew into so official an organization that it even incorporated a political anti-Semitism into its very life. Far better to have kept up friendly relations with its parental home. The modern world might have been spared some of its racial animosities, and the Church spared its repudiation at the hands of the Jews.

The early Church soon came to possess a unique character. It had no buildings, no paid clergymen, no choirs, no New Testament, no official boards, no elaborate creeds, no budgets, no cemeteries, no strong corporate union. It was a simple fellowship of faith in Jesus Christ as the ultimate and absolute Word of God to men. It was not a "Church," but an organic fellowship. It was thought of as a "family," the "body of Christ." It had personality. The fellowship had a divine initiative and calling; it had a basic faith structure.

It was not created by a constitution, nor a philosophy, nor a code of ethics. It resulted from a divine enthusiasm initiated by God's self-revelation. It was not based upon the ideal of the "brotherhood of man," nor was it a voluntary group of individuals practicing the "principles" of Jesus. Nor was it a group of reformed moralists seeking socially to reform the world. Rather, they were men and women to whom Jesus Christ had made a fundamental difference in outlook and purpose of life. But that did not imply that all Christians in the Church were alike. Their unity was in the objects of their faith and trust. As such, the Church had a peculiar form. It fed upon a certain food. It became, in time, a group that was peculiar unto itself, without giving up any of its human attributes.

Fortunately or unfortunately, that simple fellowship soon became too large to remain a fellowship. It took on the form of organization. Buildings had to be provided for its housing. The early apostles were passing away, others had to occupy their places as spiritual leaders in the Churches, and they had to be men who stood in some spiritual relation and position to the apostles. Certain habits developed, such as singing, and soon hymns came into existence. The same was true of forms of worship, church architecture, prayers, sermons and the like.

Pressure from the world without, as well as from the thinking world within (for Greek thinkers now became Christians), forced the Church to define its faith in terms of current Greek thought. Creeds resulted. There came the need for an authentic group of facts regarding Jesus' life. In the light of the many spurious Gospels that began to circulate, the

New Testament canon was formed, of course, over a period of years. The need for some corporate unity caused the churches to draw together and the ancient catholic Church arose. Soon large synodical gatherings took place, properties were acquired, and other practices spontaneously developed as the groups' experiences crystallized.

To climax it all, the State in the fourth century adopted Christianity as the official religion, and the little fellowship that once had been free and *naïve* took on the atmosphere of a huge and somewhat worldly organization, with officials richly garbed and highly honored. It seemed as if the outer structure of the Church were becoming master of the inner reality. Especially was this true in the western section of the Roman Empire, where many factors made the Church catholic into a rigid institution, unlike the earlier catholic fellowship. From then on the Church developed radicals and enthusiasts, who from time to time protested against its officialism, even as Jesus had protested against the Church of His day. The history of the later Middle Ages is the story of many protesting groups and individuals who followed in the line of Montanus and the Montanists, who desired a Church free from worldly pomp and true to the lowly Jesus; a Church whose reality would consist in purity, service, and simplicity. Against the Church of *man* they contended for a Church of *God*.

The Protestant Reformers, as well as the later protesters within Protestantism, desired a restoration or reformation of the Church. They did not desire to leave *the* Church. They desired a true Church. But they saw that outer clericalism, officialism, ecclesiasticism, formalism had been substituted for inner fellowship, true faith, obedience, and the Church's true task. Christ, the Word's authority had been assumed by ambitious churchmen who thought they were temporal vicars of Christ on earth. Christ lost His voice and His power even in His Church, amidst the voices of men who wanted Him only to substantiate their own arbitrary or erroneous ways.

It is not only against the Roman Catholic Church of the Middle Ages that protesters have agitated. They have protested against the Church in every age, Protestant and Catholic alike. Whenever the Church of God has been made a Church of man, and thereby God has lost His sovereign Lordship in His Church through His Word; whenever the Bible and its inherent living Word of God have been obscured by ecclesiastical interpretation; whenever the institutional Church has become an end in itself; whenever the Christ of the Christian faith has become distant and officially mediated by human systems; whenever the free grace of God has been dispensed by a Church which regarded itself as its only and official custodian; whenever the clergy have become a proud inhuman caste; whenever the portrayal of the message of redemption, whether in sermon or mass, has become a dead formalism or a mystic superstition instead of a witness—then the Church has been attacked, and rightly so, by *the* Church.

It is against this background that we must understand the rise of strong Reformers within the Church,
as well as radical enemies without the Church. Communism and Fascism are scourges that have arisen
because the Church has failed to be sincere and to do
its task. (Of course, that is not the whole truth.)
Likewise, heretics have arisen within the churches
because the Church has veered from its true function. Christian Science and Pentecostalism have
arisen because the Church has neglected vital elements of the Christian faith. By themselves, the
former is not realistic as to the nature of sin, while
the latter is not realistic as to the nature of God's
sovereignty. The Protestant Reformation was,
therefore, not the only attempt to restore the
medieval Church in the light of a fresh discovery of
what the Church was meant to be in the mind of
God. That discovery was made when men read the
original Bible, and therein discovered the com-
munion ideal of the early Church, full of simplicity
and sincerity and the realism of a faith in a sharing
God.

As such, the Protestant Reformation was not a
revolt against *the* Church but only against its false
nature. To the Reformers the medieval Church was
anti-Christian. They did not wish to divide the
Church into churches. They wanted to redeem the
Church from its errors and to reconstruct, or reform,
it in the light of its true nature as a Church of God.
It was only after all efforts at reconciliation had
failed that they reluctantly consented to re-found

the Church as a Church restored according to the Word of God. Politics entered to sharpen religious differences. Other factors, economic and national, assisted in making the Protestant leaders align themselves with rising social and economic forces. That tragic, but perhaps unavoidable, act of division opened the way for all the numerous churches we today possess.

Again, it is unfortunate that Protestantism has not maintained a closer interest in the ancient Catholic Church. We might have been spared many of the Protestant-Catholic animosities of our modern world. For, to some, a "Protestant" is merely an anti-Catholic, and to others, a "Catholic" is merely an anti-Protestant. While we may not agree, the door should always remain open for that larger comradeship which the Church so sorely needs in this age of social movements that possess a solidarity undergirded by religious and fanatical realism.

Of course the Protestant Reformation was not complete, nor could it be. The early idealistic intentions of the Reformers, as of all reformers, soon were modified by the existing status of life. Men then lived in a relative world, as do we. The Reformers realized that they could succeed only in so far as they allied themselves with rising social forces, which at that time were nations and the middle or merchant capitalistic classes. As a result, on the one hand, the Protestant churches became allied with nations, and the national churches were founded.

In some respects this "entangling alliance" has

been good; especially for that age. It gave the
infant Church a strong national protection in the
face of many dangerous enemies. It gave the
Church a social prestige. It has also made religious
education a part of the national educational policy.
Ministers received training in larger university centers. Churches were formed on a community basis,
and no duplication of effort was allowed. And religion was given a social value, which made it possible
for all citizens of the State to have at least a minimum
religious training. As a result, royalty and the
churches were wedded, creeds or symbols were made
at the emperors' behest. "Altar" and "Throne"
went together.

While these may be values, the disadvantage has
been that such national churches have weakened the
unity of the universal Church. Churches were made
subservient to the conscience and culture of the human State. A religion that is a social function soon
loses its evangelistic zeal, its intelligence, its true
Gestalt, and the energy born of struggle to maintain
its independence. The Christianity of a State
Church is denatured of its radical and critical temper.
The alliance drags the Church into wars prosecuted
for national honor. The unique theological base of
the Church's message is denied or denatured. The
Christianity of such a Church is diluted to a merely
cultural plane, and its ethics is forced to adjust itself
to the national group. While it may provide a
minimum religious training for the whole nation,
many doubt whether that advantage is better than

the other alternative, where a free Church provides a virile maximum religious life for the interested few.

A classic illustration of the plight of a national Church is to be found in Germany, where for centuries the Church has allied itself with the culture and national aspirations of a race of people which today is fighting for its independence and for cultural and racial unity. The State is expecting the Church to support its political aims, claiming that these aims are right and Christian. What will result no one knows. It would mean another revolution with loss of property and prestige for clergy and churches alike, were the Protestant churches which are so closely linked with the economic and cultural side of German life to declare their independence. (Such an event took place in Scotland in 1843, when the United Free Church of Scotland left the State Church.)

But there have been other "unholy alliances" which have robbed the Protestant Church of its true nature. If the Reformers were justified in their desire to restore the true nature of the Church, it is also true that their withdrawal from the Roman Catholic Church, and their insistence upon individualism, have not only given us State churches, but churches in which an atomizing individualism, and a middle-class culturalism, have worked havoc with the true nature of the Church. Our sectarian American churches may be more of a liability than national churches, in the long run.

There is no doubt that Protestantism has been predominant in lands where great economic and physical progress has taken place. Protestant churches became, in many instances, class churches, where the social scale of members played a part in the life of the Church. Dr. H. Richard Niebuhr, of Yale University, in an interesting study of this problem,[1] has revealed that the wealthy classes as a rule belong to stately churches, while the poorer classes adhere to the enthusiastic sect-type of Christian fellowships. Protestantism's close relation to middle-class *bourgeois* culture has robbed the Church of a wider appeal, and has made it a Church of respectable people, who live conventionally decent Christian lives. In fact, however, Protestant churches are often morally snobbish and pharisaical.

Other things have disrupted the true nature of the Church within Protestantism. *Human standards* of biblical interpretation have been made dogmatically final, and, as a result, many Protestant churches are more nearly exclusive, sectarian churches of men's standards and interpretations than churches of the Gospel of God. Or, churchmen, especially fond of intellectualism, have unconsciously made intellectual standards and shibboleths the measuring rod of the Church, and thereby have limited the Church of God to a select group.

There have also been pietist groups whose inner experience, emotional reactions, or even their clothes,

---

[1] *Social Sources of Denominationalism.* Henry Holt & Company, New York.

have been made the final standard in the Church. Subjective reactions have usurped the place of the objective producer of the experience. The means is substituted for the end, or, rather, the experience is made primary at the expense of the experience-producer. And those who do not have a peculiar "feeling" or "Spirit experience" are dechurched, and dechristianized. Some churchmen make the social application of the gospel a plumb line, and as a result the Church is narrowed down to a mere society for the melioration of social maladjustments. Or, the Church may become, as it often has in Protestant circles, an incohesive bundle of "spiritual" individuals, who set up enthusiastic individualism as the last thing in the Christian faith.

All of these standards, or human limitations, of the Church's true nature have been set up by one denomination or another within the Protestant fold. They have their *relative* places. The Church of God becomes a Church of man, and the human interpretations, human reactions, or human judgments have taken precedence over the God of the Church when they become absolute criteria. There is little distinction between the human officialism of the Roman Catholic Church and the human subjectivism and humanism of the Protestant churches. The Church, in any case, suffers at the hands of the church*es* and church*men*. Humanism, in one form or another, has ran away with the Church. The true fellowship of Christian people in Christ has been abducted by zealous, idolatrous, and avaricious humanity. The one holy catholic Church has been crucified in the house of its so-called friends.

Protestant humanism has, of course, done its good work. It has given us towering Christian personalities. It has enhanced the human side of life. It has made it possible for the world to experience progress in the fields of philosophy, science, economics, and politics. But, when it arrives at an *impassé* because of its sheer atomism, when it makes an unholy alliance with nations, middle-class culture and smug pharisaism, it robs itself of its independence, and robs the world of the true objective reality of the Church and of the true community which the Church is to demonstrate to a divided and suffering world. This is tragic for God and for the world.

There are many who would say that our present social distress is in great part due to humanistic Protestantism. For it has undergirded our individualism and our nationalism with spiritual sanctions. As a result, the Western world no longer knows the meaning of "community." Individualism has atomized the social order. It has created a generation of individualistic people who have been preying upon society only for their selfish profit, or preying upon the Church for their personal spiritual profit. Whereas, there can be no true individualism without a society. Man as a unit cannot live in a vacuum; he must live in an organism as cells live in a body. So there can be no Christian individual without a Christian community. Protestantism's alliance with *bourgeois*, or individualistic, culture has not only been its own undoing, but is the cause of inward moral decay in Western society.

The national Church has the tendency to lose its nature as a Christian community, based upon Christ, by making the Christian community commensurate with the national group, and by accepting the dangerous prestige that such an alliance gives. On the other hand, the individualistic or sectarian Church provincializes its Christian community by appeals to peculiar human interpretations, cultural or racial groups. In short, the Word of God, which is meant to be the unitive and authoritative factor in the Church, is soon displaced by human elements, and the Church loses its unitive authority in the gospel, and finally, its fellow-feeling, its catholicity. Sectarian Christianity, especially that found in the individualistic churches, has produced a Christianity unduly concerned with individual Christian experience, intellectual definitions, ethical codes, and the like. The idea of *the* Church is then dissolved. The Church, in that case, becomes merely a place where an aggregation of individuals come to have their souls revived and fed, or to be substantiated in their bourgeois decency, or *their* religious ideas.

The danger of Roman Catholicism is that it mechanizes and externalizes the Church; the danger of Protestantism is that it individualizes and atomizes the Church. Catholicism institutionalizes the Church; Protestantism subjectivizes the Church. In either case the Church is humanized. It is at the mercy of man.

It is quite evident today that men are seeking a new community ideal. "Communism" and "Fascism" are terms that describe movements bent on producing social unity. Great social forces are at work in our modern world, undergirded by sincere, even fanatic, religious dynamic, to have a new world of social solidarity regardless of the individual or of common laws of liberal tolerance. Pagan religions are taking on new forces everywhere, and they are appropriating to themselves the *outer* tasks of the Church, in the *forms* of social service, personal religion, and the like.

The Church is today meeting these forces in a head-on collision. Both Fascism and Communism regard the Church as a factor to be dealt with in the creation of their ideas as to what a community should be. Both are secular faiths. And the Church is beginning to sense its need for discovering its basis of existence in order to save its soul as well as its treasure of truth regarding the true nature of man and God. The coming battle will not be about external forms so much as about *theology*. The Church needs to retrace some of its steps in order to see where the thread of its true nature began to be lost. Perhaps that thread was lost when it began to lose its sense of dependence upon its true Lord. It sought to establish its community and fellowship upon another basis than upon *the Christ* upon whom it first rested. It exalted secondary things to primary importance. National prestige, human interpretations and experiences, alliances with the "world" in the hope that thereby it might become great—these and all their attendant evils have weakened rather than strengthened the Church. If the Roman Catholic Church loses its strength by making itself the direct spokesman of God on earth, forgetting its servitude as a sinful institution, perhaps the Protestant Church does the same thing in another direction, by likewise forgetting the true nature and basis of the Church.

The Church, especially in America, has come to serve "progress," or democracy, or *bourgeois* capitalistic culture; man, and not God alone. (And progress, democracy, and even freedom, can be thoroughly immoral!) Churches have become divided on the bases of race, of social position, of cultural groups. They have sought to serve the world as they thought the world *wanted* to be served. Secularistic ideas have crept into the Church, and the standards of the world have been adopted as the accepted standards. There may be truth in the statement that the secularism which the Jerusalem missionary conference of 1928 regarded as the arch enemy of Christianity is only the "false sanctity" of an apostate Church coming to plague its mother! The inward holiness of the Church is an assumed holiness. There is a hollowness at the heart of the Church. It lacks the essential note of a divine meaningfulness and seriousness about its task.

This shallow or superficial attitude regarding the deeper nature of the Church has been especially evident in our modern scientific world. Life was regarded in terms of things and external standards. In America the voluntary principle in church life made churches work to win adherents, and to raise money for the Church's maintenance. In the rush of such activities, the deeper elements involved in quiet evangelism and the essential nature of the Church were innocently and unconsciously relegated to the side.

Thus the human side of the Church was magnified. The "minister became an administer." Busyness was substituted for reality, activity for inward being. The churches became congeries of ambitious organizations, often working without any unified sense of direction or church-consciousness. Big business methods were introduced into church affairs. Efficiency was stressed. Religious education, in its early stages at least, was regarded as the one great program for the elimination of crime and for the controlled education of children that would produce a Christian America in a short time. It lacked theological depth, and neglected the idea of the Church. Churches were regarded as good social institutions, and men were invited to join the church for what the church would do for *them*, and for what their allegiance to the church would do *for* the welfare of the community. Even missions promoted the idea that the world could be Christianized by man in one generation, and Christianity was often interpreted as a body of truths that could socially reconstruct the world.

Worship became a lost art, for it no longer sought

to celebrate objectively God's worth and sovereignty; it sought to exalt the subjective states of man by songs and "peppy" talks. Topical sermons abounded. Spicy themes were the order of the day. People came to church to hear the *preacher*. They were permitted to become members on their own terms. They were sprayed with moralizations from the pulpit, in the hope that the humanitarian sympathy of Jesus might "take" and they would go out to be decent people. The deep realism of the Gospels was toned down to a shallow idealism of the Golden Rule, the brotherhood of man, and the Fatherhood of God. Churches sought to entertain people timidly, and their high religion of demand was diluted to suit the whims of worshipers. The churches became humanly inflated at the expense of the church's theological assets.

Benevolent work was often mechanized and isolated from the work of the Church. Its administration-board experts who "promoted" the work, divorced these interests from the local church. In some respects the office of the ministry has been cheapened by the minister's desire to be popular or ultrahuman. Sunday-school work, which is considered an auxiliary work of the Church, in many cases runs away with the Church or becomes a poor substitute for the Church in promoting a kind of Christianity that can hardly be distinguished from an ethical Pollyannaism which defeats the growth of virile faith and reverent worship. Many of our churches are so cluttered with a multitude of ambitious organizations that it is impossible to say what the Church is!

This trend of the Church toward a dilution of its true nature has its counterpart in every department of its life. One has but to look at the church colleges, once stanchly grounded in the radical nature of Christian theology, but which now, as institutions of higher learning far removed from their constituencies by great endowments, are scarcely distinguishable from State schools in atmosphere and curriculum. Most of them are liabilities to the Church at large.

We have lived through a period of excessive church building, much of which was unnecessary and disastrous. It was due largely to human pride, building external structures that did not have enough inward reality and power to sustain them, depression or no depression. Today the churches face enervating debts that lead them to resort to the queerest activities to make money. The church thus enslaved financially, soon loses its power of independence.

Evangelism and stewardship, necessary and vital elements in Christian faith, are often carried on, not in good faith, nor in the spirit of humble faith, but for the purpose of enhancing the number of members and increasing the donations to support the overorganized church work. As a result of these various influences at work, especially upon the modern Protestant churches, it is evident that through a concern for the external side of the Church, the Western world has become a world with a great vacuum at the core of life. The Church's salt, while not altogether lost, is quite stale. The Church, as a custodian of the very throne of life, has evacuated its position. (Perhaps it was aware of its false gospel, which it secretly distrusted as absolute!) It has been disastrous not only to the world but to the Church. If Communism and Fascism today represent social collectivisms with religious dynamics, it is because they are feeding upon the primal urge of man for a loyalty to something higher than himself, something which he can enthrone in his heart, and upon the deep desire of man for social unity and security based upon a religious reality.

It is for these reasons that the Church is regarded by many as an extra organization to join, as a preaching station for morality, as a busy organization, an isolated kill-joy group which constantly pours "cold water" on good intentions; or as a group of spiritually peculiar egoists who sit in judgment upon sinners. Some regard the Church as a *bourgeois* institution aimed to maintain an individualistic culture.

It is this stigma that the Church must refute, not with words, although they are necessary, but with reality, and a return to "first principles." The conflict confronting the Church clearly indicates the stand it will need to make. And its first task is not to *do* something spectacular, not to listen to the world, but to examine itself in quietness, to repent of its prodigality and to seek that stamina and that power which come of perfect obedience to its true

Lord and purpose. It must give a sincere witness to its central Reality.

Perhaps the term "church" will need to be re-defined. It should be replaced with the word "community," or the term "place," for the Church is the Christian community, or brotherhood, created by the sovereign Word of God. It is God's "place" in men's lives. The Church is not, therefore, fundamentally a human institution. It has a divine origin and function. It exists because Jesus Christ lived and because He brought something that by its very nature draws into community those who associate with Him. It exists because God will have His will and word known. It is Jesus Christ who makes the Christian community, not on the basis of what the community *decides* or *experiences*, but upon the basis of what that community *learns* from Him. The Church is not an association of people who are interested in "religion," or even social betterment. It is primarily a company of people who have been apprehended by God in Christ, and who associate together in the spirit of common humility and service.

The Church is not the clergy, nor the members, nor the pronouncements of the official Church. It is that cross-section of human society where the Lord God and Father of Jesus Christ is taken seriously, where men live not by their own religious ideas but repentantly by God's ideas, judgment, and love. People in the Church do not live by illusions as to their own goodness or moral perfection. They live derived lives, their whole beings sensitized by the

Lordship of God in Christ. They are not just decent people; they are sinners saved by the love of God, and who affirm life as and where it is in the power of God.

As such the Church is not a group of religious intellectuals, nor perfect moralists, nor emotional mystics. The human side of the Church is a cross-section of sinners. For that reason the true Church (which includes the ministry) does not isolate itself from sinful men. On the contrary, it is not alien to everything that is human. It is not a preacher's Church, nor a Church lost in numerous groups of human interests. Its life is derived from the grace of God and the whole Word of God, which gives the Church its constant power and sustaining reality in the midst of all sorts of men.

The Church, then, is a cross-section of humanity as it is, and no true Church would deny the existence of Church beyond the boundaries of the organized churches, nor deny the existence of the "world" in the Church. For a Church is not a group of divinized individuals, nor is it a mystic and esoteric cult. Rather, it is a society of real people in which the true purpose of God is at work in the realm "world." The Church cannot be limited or defined.

But that should not deny to the human side of the Church some relative significance. The outer life of the Church must seek always to conform to its inner reality. And yet, the human Church is always relative, sinful, full of varying degrees of capacities and developments in people, under the judgment of God, because it too is "world." But unity, authority, discipline, and order should be its ideals. This side of the Church must be enhanced in Protestantism. But it dare not go so far as to materialize its gospel in an external ecclesiastical conformity. To do so is to identify the Church with the Word of God. The human side of the Church must always be critically related to the true Church of God.

There are many Protestant ministers, among them this writer, who would have little quarrel with the Roman Catholic Church, were it not for the Roman doctrine of "temporal sovereignty," which practically identifies the external Church with God. If the Roman Catholic Church were to maintain a spiritual catholicity, we should have little trouble with unity. The danger of the Church, when seeking to become a manifest divine institution in the world, with temporal power in the world, is that it makes itself worldly and loses its real power, which comes of obedience to divine authority. A Church which has temporal sovereignty is one that the powers of this world can defeat, since it takes on the same character as that of a modern society. The Church, in the Protestant interpretation of the term, is a Church under the cross, not externally militant in its own power, but inwardly militant in the power of the Word of God which is beyond human control or attack. The Church's power does not reside in its human qualities. The Church is always a mighty force in the world when it is weak in its human side but strong in its obedience to God.

When Luther burned the papal bull in Wittenberg, he not only defied the Church's power over his dynamic individual experience, but he burned the code of the canon law, in which the Church of that day proposed to *legislate* for and dictate to *all* human relations of life. Such a Church has become a State, he thought. The true Church will make itself powerful only as it refuses earthly pomp and power and looks upon itself as part of the world which has become aware of God's gospel in the midst of normal life. No Church that selfishly expects the world to come into its membership to be saved, can hope to be saved itself. With such a conception of the Church in the life of Protestantism, one can see that *the* Church is beyond the churches and their nonessential differences. The strength and the power and the unity of the Church lie not in human hands but in God's hands. *No movement for unity can succeed if the power of obedience to Him is lacking.*

True, forms of organization, tempers of denominations, individual experiences, types of worship will continue to vary. But over and above that is the compelling dynamic of that which lies beyond these forms of expression. If static organic unity of uniformity is not desirable, or possible, within Protestantism, we can do our common task, and make our common corporate witness through federated agencies which can take on vital theological character, and as expedient agencies do our common task. The Church has no desire to *control* the world, but to redeem it, and you cannot redeem it by beating it into conformity. God's salvation does not make stereotyped robots, but followers. No human Church dare hope to control the world so long as the human Church is always a part of the "world."

The world awaits this Christian community which transcends our racial, national, and class barriers. It may not be conscious of it, but the world waits. Even the churches await the coming of the Church. The churches cannot go on loyal to two masters. A universal fellowship of Christians, obedient to a common God, would provide the womb out of which could be born the new humanity. The new humanity must be born to stave off disaster. It *must* be if there is a God. For the Church to give a living, sincere witness to *that* would be for her to give the greatest witness of God this world would know!

But to do this something decisive and critical is needed. The Churches must repent! They must make the "great refusal" to the bid for worldly popularity or power. They must withdraw from the world inwardly, so as to understand why there is a Church and what its chief function is. The Church must recover its solidarity, its willingness to be done with earthly pomp, and assume a cross. It must rediscover and proclaim with absolute certainty the greatness and the totalitarianism of its Christ. It must see that its power does not inhere in its *subjective experience* but in its *objective imperative*. It must become vibrant and sensitive to the problems of life as concerns with which God has everything to do, and must give birth to heralds who shall invade life with the mandate from God, and who under the Lordship of God will do what *can* be done in a relative situation. It must not seek to become an end in itself, in this day when both the temptation to withdraw from the world, and to gain egotistical control of the world is everywhere so strong. When that idea emerges in the minds of churchmen, the day of the artificial and damnable distinction between laity and clergy will be past. The day of the distinction between the "visible" and the "invisible" Church will be gone, as will the day of the fateful distinction between the Church and the "world."

The Church of Jesus Christ will survive, for God's mandate unto men cannot be hid under a bushel. He will summon others to proclaim His right and His claim to the lives of men and the possessions of the world. It behooves the modern Church to sacrifice external glory and numbers for the greater glory of absolute obedience.

But the earthly and sinful side of that Church's life will needs suffer alterations as ages change and ages emerge. The Church's reason for existence is greater and larger than the human side of the Church, and it is only as the human side of the Church stays true to the divine side that it can hope to live and be a force in the life of man and society. To do that it must be a true servant, a true witness to the unique truth that is its only justification for existence and its assumption of the name of a Church of Christ.

No brilliant intellectual apologetics, no ecclesiastical program, no high direct social action, no scientific religious education, no artificial propagation of causes and of "stewardship," no sheer activism, no ecclesiastical politics, no traditional dogmatism, no humanistic ethic, no arbitrary catholicity can save the Church now. There is nothing left but lowly obedience, the "ancient sacrifice," the cross. The Church will be saved to bless when it strikes its breast and confesses itself a sinner. In that day of weakness, it shall be the strongest power in the world, a power to which men will listen.

For those who always ask, "Well, now what shall we *do?*" there is only a rebuke. They have not seen the crisis of the Church. It is not a matter of following a blue-print, but of attaining an attitude. The hard task remains, namely, to stop mistaking the outer structure of the Church for the inward nature. *We* humans cannot build the Church. God builds it where His Word is proclaimed sincerely and men in faith accept it in obedience. That Word will validate itself, and make for a Church that will be a true Church. When that attitude comes to churchmen, they will no longer fear for the future of *the* Church in whatever form it may survive. They will fear only lest their own unfaithfulness shall fail to give a true witness to the central truth of the Church.

Such a church will possess an inner life that will have power to shame sinners to repentance; to lead into greater truth; to give life eternal meaningfulness; and to make calculating worldliness and self-sufficiency flee. Only an obedient Church can hope for survival. For any other kind of Church there is no survival.

When the Church recovers its feeling of oneness in the truth, and with it of corporate obedience to the truth, there will be a new day in American church life. Instead of the varieties of agencies now at work on so many different things, all of which are good, the Church will be able to do its work through constituent agencies that will be backed by the corporate power of the Church. As it is, Christian education, temperance action, evangelism, peace promotion, and general social action are carried on by too many unrelated agencies. They live an atomistic and fragmentary existence either at the hands of the denominations or at the hands of federated bodies. They lack oneness of Christian purpose, found alone in the Church.

In the early Church the organization had many functions, all of them considered legitimate, from prophecy and healing to taking care of the poor. None of these varied agencies regarded their work as either more or less important, and none were divorced from the true witness of the Church. The central Truth was, of course, determinant, but all other expressions were branches on the same vine. This is the sort of unity needed in American churches and it is doubtful whether it will ever be achieved unless we see the need for the recovery of the Church catholic. Such a Superchurch would not be a new Church, but a corporate body of definitely delegated authority, the achievement of which would involve the downright relinquishing of absolute autonomy on the part of the denominations in favor of a necessary higher absolute autonomy.

Such a Church would not eradicate the churches. It would give them their only hope for continued existence.

CHAPTER VIII

WHO IS JESUS CHRIST?

THE nature of Jesus Christ is the essence of the Christian religion. In a real sense Christianity either stands or falls with Him. And since Protestantism has staked its all on the word of God revealed finally in Jesus Christ, and not on the ecclesiastical institution, nor on an appeal to the infallible Bible, it needs to make sure of His authority, especially in the light of the free inquiry which the critics have been making into His life.

There is much confusion in Protestant circles as to the significance and meaning of Jesus in the Christian faith. Not that Protestant leaders ignore Jesus, or think Him irrelevant or antedated. It is, rather, a confusion regarding His nature, His relation to God, His right to speak for the absolute God, and some uncertainty that He is the only Saviour. There is no unity of witness which would give the world to think that Christ is of God and not of man. Our world is not made to feel the absolute God-in-action in Jesus. His office as Mediator between God and man has been largely replaced in our thought by His office as a "religious" Example or pioneer of "religion."

The sharp paradoxical Christology of the fathers is no longer playing a leading rôle in the churches. Jesus has been made more human, to be sure. But the objective, mysterious, sovereign, and decisive element in His historic meaning has been subtly softened except in certain centers, and in these centers the doctrine of Christ is made more a matter of dogmatic definitions than of living theology. This orthodox Christology is not adapted to modern thought and it serves a reactionary Christianity.

The loss of this mysterious transcendence in Jesus Christ is a, if not *the*, problem of American Protestantism. This has been due primarily to two causes. Man has toned down the nature of sin from innate guilt which separates him from God and which tinges all his actions, even including his goodness, to the idea of sin as a mere ignorance of the right or an impediment in human nature which will be eliminated through educational processes. On the other hand, man has toned God down from a transcendent and righteous God to an immanent process within nature which comes to fullest evolutionary development in man, especially in human geniuses, specifically in Jesus the Genius. As a result there is no longer need of a strong Christ to bridge a chasm which man cannot bridge by his own effort, and which God alone can bridge only at the cost of His infinite love in a marvelous sharing of Himself in a special action for and among men. It was upon this basis that our fathers spoke of Jesus Christ as both God and Man. The very words "Jesus Christ" are paradoxical. Jesus means the human, and Christ the divine, or God side, of the One who is the center of Christian faith and revelation.

The problem of American Protestantism lies not in its emphasis upon the historical and human side of Jesus' life, but, rather, in the fact that it has allowed this side of Jesus Christ to take prominence at the expense of the "other" element in Him, which was far more important.

There have been forces at work, especially in the field of historical criticism, religious psychology, and religious history, which have tended to dissolve the uniqueness of Jesus Christ. We have already mentioned the this-worldly interest of men in general. The kingdom of God hence came to be interpreted more in terms of an evolving world of abundant life for all, which it was Jesus' sole concern to bring to pass, abundant life meaning a "terrestrial Messianism" of course—all those comforts and conveniences that would make *this* life complete and free from restraints material and spiritual.

The study of comparative religions tended to take away the absoluteness of Jesus Christ and the uniqueness of Christianity. Psychology began to interpret personality in terms of complexes, and the term "sin" was applied to those "maladjustments" of soul which might be eliminated by psychic tricks and remedies, or by more education. The history of religions revealed that Christianity was very much like other religions, except that it brought the desires of other religions to a better fruition. At least Christianity was like other religions in kind.

Slowly men began to adopt the idealistic view of life. The tragedy of sin was ignored. Human reason was regarded as an expression of the divine creative Spirit in man. Christ's divinity resided, so some said, in His God-consciousness, His greater development of that divine mind which is native to all men. Thus, Jesus was made a pioneer in the development of *man's* innate God-consciousness. He was *of* us. His "deity" was no longer spoken of, but men spoke of His "divinity," by which they meant His divine humanity. He was the truest symbol of the divine in man. Jesus gave human beings fullness of natural life. The authority of Jesus was in His power to *make men divine*. This is a far cry from the older doctrine of Jesus Christ as the Mediator between sinful man and a righteous God. In that doctrine man needed more than mere education, more than a high human example for his salvation. He needed redemption which he could not create, but which he must receive at the hands of a God whose miraculous nature was self-giving love. And that love and redemption was declared to us in Jesus, the Christ.

Those who gave us this more humanistic conception of Jesus are not to be condemned utterly. They did their work well. They dealt a blow to the older and untenable theological dualism. They made Christ real, and a factor in actual human life. No longer was He the cold medieval Christ. They disregarded the old debates about the "nature" or "essence" of Christ, and placed great emphasis upon the social character of Christianity. They released the faith from static literalism and magnified the ethical side of Christianity. They dignified human reason with co-operative powers with God. They liberated man from the slavery of scholasticism and showed that God's revelation operated not so much through rational deductions of theologians as through practical life and simple faith.

It is in the extreme and popular development of this trend that the real problem of our American Protestantism lies. In this we have sinned more than have others. Jesus has been made into a mere utilitarian technique for the fullest expression of *human* life as it is. Little thought has been paid to the crisis of the older conversion experience, in which Jesus Christ confronted men with the demand for absolute repentance and faith. Thus the modern liberal Christ has been made a pragmatic "Jesus of history," a means toward man's development, a tool for our ends, an easy Comrade with men. The American Jesus has been shorn of His high dignity by our unwarranted familiarity with His terrible divine sincerity and earnestness.

This emphasis upon Jesus as a human genius in things religious came simultaneously with the rise of man in every realm of life, through the invention of machines and the control of nature by his genius. An optimistic attitude prevailed regarding the nature of man. Education was considered the scientific means of eradicating from man those outgrown vestiges of his former self. Sin was ignorance. Idealism and positivism and the doctrine of evolution all enhanced the natural powers of man. "Religion" too was considered something native to man in his God-consciousness, and all things religious originated therein. Even theology became an empirical science of the human God-consciousness, instead of a critical rethinking of the objective meaning of God's revelation in Jesus Christ.

In the United States, where man advanced scientifically to a most remarkable degree, this would naturally have its greatest practical development. Churches here enhanced man's experience. Here churches were in the hands of laymen who wanted a "going" type of Christianity. Here religion could do things in the social world. Thus the aim of the Christian religion was identified with human betterment, with human progress, and the coming of democracy was considered proof of the coming of the kingdom of God. Modern conveniences were likewise interpreted as results of the coming of the Kingdom. Thus Jesus Christ was humanized. Today this liberal, optimistic, and simple idea of Jesus is having great difficulty in maintaining itself. Not only does it repudiate the very Christology of the New Testament and of those who founded the faith in the absoluteness of Jesus Christ, but it is impotent to meet the situation which the Church faces both in the world and in its own household. A purely otherworldly Christ is as utterly unsatisfactory as is a purely this-worldly Jesus. The two belong together.

This humanistic Jesus leads us straight to a worldview that certainly is not Christian. While Christian revelation does not give us a detailed metaphysics, cosmology, and the like, it surely does give us a world-view based upon the real natures of God and man. Christianity stands or falls with its idea of sin as being the real problem in the relation of God to life and society. In this realm of unrighteousness Christ is Mediator and authority. But to say that there is no disruption here, is to say that Christ is not Mediator and Redeemer in the historic Christian sense.

This picture of Jesus dilutes the drastic nature of man's sin and disobedience, and makes Jesus to be only an ethical teacher and not a Redeemer from that awful sin which drives a wedge between man and his God. Such a concept of Jesus denies the need for a radical revelation which the Bible presupposes on every page. Further, it practically eliminates the deep and decisive nature of the atonement and makes of the cross of Christ something less terrible than it meant to Jesus Himself. By diluting the nature of sin, it makes God and man to be closely identified, and by softening the chasm between a righteous God and unrighteous man it runs into an easy monistic idealism, a naturalistic pantheism which is hardly any better than Plato's idealism. Above all, it disposes of the idea of the coming of Jesus Christ as the great good news from God. It denies the need for strong divine grace to give men power to live with the meaning of God in their lives. The nature of Jesus is consequently diluted to the plane of a natural man whose genius in religion may be high, but who is not a Redeemer in the Christian sense of the word. Such a world-view, which is nothing more than a high idealism, loses sight of the second person in the Trinity, which is distinctive to Christianity. That doctrine is a functional explanation of the fact that God is more than a cold and static Being, Creator, or World-All; He is a God who loves and moves toward man, and in the Holy Spirit completes in us the work He has begun in the Son of God.

So simplified an idea of Jesus does not at all harmonize with the absolute statements about Him in the New Testament, or in the historic faith. This modern concept of Jesus has been largely read into the New Testament by ourselves. We read Him in the light of our own desires. We made Him say what we wanted Him to say. This Jesus is largely man's creation under the spell of his romanticism and his optimistic idealism. The sterner elements in the life of Jesus were eradicated or explained away. His absoluteness and aloofness were sweetened to our own taste. Jesus came to be tacked onto our own thinking as we add an annex to a house. He became the kind of religious Leader we wanted Him to be— a social Reformer, a Teacher of "religious ideals" like other teachers, or an intensifier of our own "religious consciousness." Such a picture of Jesus has robbed Him of His absoluteness, His right to be Himself, and His sovereign reality which never meets man as sinful man wants Jesus to meet him. Thus, the real Jesus has largely become a product of man, the servant of man, and not the Lord of life, God's producer of a new man.

It was not science as such that did all this. Science has its legitimate place. The pride of man dissolved the sinful ethical chasm that separates man from God. Man would gladly try to make himself better than he really is. Thus Jesus Christ lost His high divine nature which approached lost man to redeem him utterly, and in the place of lost man is substituted an optimistic, Pelagian idea of man as one who is slowly but surely, by his own powers, approximating God. Thus God is made into man's image, even the high God who meets us in a living and personal way in Jesus Christ. This explains, in part, how biblical historical science repudiated what are thought to be the outworn ideas of Jesus' apocalypticism and eschatology. Biblical scientists either ignored these phases of Jesus' life, or "explained" them away as mental frameworks of the gospel which were part of the first-century world-view. Many have said that since we no longer believe in that mental framework, we can discard both the apocalypticism and the eschatology of Jesus.

True, we can no longer hold to the mental outlook of the old Greeks and Hebrews. We no longer believe in a flat earth, and we no longer live in a simple prescientific age. But let us not be too sure that apocalypticism and eschatology are to be discarded in their entirety. They were fundamental in the mind of Jesus, and let us not forget that the early Church held to the idea of the return of Jesus Christ. True, they may have been mistaken as to the time. But the idea of the return of Jesus Christ, which means the sure and future coming of *God's* kingdom, is not an outworn fact in the faith. Beneath it there is a profound truth.

The same is true of apocalypticism. To discard these in their first-century forms is one thing. But to discard their inner meanings is quite another; it cannot be done without tearing something out of the context of the total faith. (And Christian faith and doctrine is a unit, since all of its doctrines hang together, and to speak of one, such as the atonement, is to speak of all the others, even the incarnation, the consummation, etc.)

Today we are bewildered by our cheap church success and illusory popularity. The world is weary of sentiment, illusions, and man-made ideals. This same world, in many sections, is turning to absolute loyalties beyond its reach. We have suffered the deflation of our optimistic conceptions of man, history, and reality. And today we churchmen are again reading the New Testament and about the Christ of the historic faith in a different light and with a different attitude. We are beginning to strike our breasts as did the prodigal and to seek the Homeland of our neglected faith. I think we will again see with more abundant enthusiasm and with more exalted vision the high doctrine of the Christ of God which gave the Church its birth, and which in history has given it the power of a triumphant faith.

"Religions" will continue, in one form or another, whether of race or class or any other idol, to plague the prodigal Church. Ideals will no longer help, for they are often only projected human objectives. Subjectivism is a poor refuge, for it only digs desperate man deeper into the insoluble problem of himself. But the solution to man's deepest problem is beyond himself, and he knows not how to find it. Mere mustard plasters in the form of moral advice do not help; they do not reach the deep disease of Church, society, and self. Analysis of the difficulty only intensifies the problem. Driven into a corner, we are fast losing the speculative bent of the spectator in our research regarding Jesus and are beginning to ask ourselves deep questions about the power and the reality in the lives of men of other days, men who faced situations similar to, if not as exasperating and chaotic as, our own. In this plight, it is not a Jesus of "ideals" that we need; nor will a man-made Christ stand the strain. We do not need a teacher of beautiful ethical idealism, who might be sufficient for a prosperous and easy age. We need a strong Christ, a Christ who, from beyond us, can become a living and eternal fulcrum for our lives and who can save.

It was not the "religion of Jesus" that started the Christian movement. Long before there were any Synoptics telling about the "life" of Jesus, there was a Christian fellowship centering in faith *in* Jesus as an absolute object of God's revelation. To those early believers, Jesus did not have the "value" of God. He made men aware of that God who is beyond human evaluations. The so-called "life" of Jesus which the historical sciences in the last century were discovering, is not a "life" in the modern sense.

The Gospels are anything but "lives," or "biographies," of Jesus. They are witnesses to the Christhood of Jesus, written by men who were not primarily interested in His humanity. All the effort expended in writing lives of Jesus, from Renan to Murray to Browne to Barton and Gibran, are interesting, but rather irrelevant. They have helped, of course. But in utilizing the "documents" to write about the man Jesus these men have neglected the very premise and background upon which these documents rest. The historical Jesus of the so-called Synoptic Gospels is not a primary datum. The primary datum concerns the Christ of God.

The historical Jesus is a Jesus who has been largely *read into* the New Testament by men living in the romantic and rationalistic modern world. The assumptions of the critical scholars are widely variant from the assumptions of the original records and faith. Some historical scholars have been honest enough to confess that they have very little evidence that can be used to construct a validly "historical" figure. For every shred of the gospel writings was written by men who believed something *about* Jesus, men who had no desire to write an impartial biography of an interesting "religious" man. Early Christians *trusted* Jesus, because He was the Christ.

Even if we discarded the Christ of Paul's Epistles, and came to such a definition of the nature of Christianity as that which Harnack gave us, namely, "the Fatherhood of God, the love of fellow men to one another, human worth and righteousness of the

heart"—then do we not have to face the problem of
the Synoptics themselves? Surely, it was faith in
Christ that preserved the Jesus of history! Thus the
impact of modern scholarship will increasingly wear
thin the old distinction between Paul and the Synoptics. The variety of religions in the New Testament
will also be increasingly seen in the light of their
unity in Christ. Paul himself was a member of the
very Christian community that wrote the Synoptics.
And the Church, or Christian community, existed
prior to the Gospels, and was founded upon *faith in
Jesus* as the Christ, an object of divine meaning.

The fourth Gospel has been called historically useless. Yet the writer wrote with the same assumptions
of faith in Jesus the Christ as did his fellow Gospel
writers, and he wrote with Christian faith still fresh
in his heart, and with a longer perspective as to the
real meaning of the Jesus the Christ in the life of the
fellowship of faith. Of course we shall not be able
to use it as primary data. No human Jesus could
have grounded the Christian Church, or community.
No human genius had that power. There is no
Socratesian Church.

In short, there never was such a thing as a pure
simple gospel centering in the "religion of Jesus."
Such a portrait of Jesus is only a reading of something romantic and alien into the reality of Jesus,
something which the early Christian fellowship never
held.

The one fundamental assumption underlying the
whole portrait of Jesus in the New-Testament Chris-

tian community is that in Jesus, God was moving toward and among men in a unique and unconditioned act. His eternal purpose was in fruition. He was doing something for men which lost men could not do for themselves, and man's true religion was not to be an attempt to *do* something for God, but to accept what God was doing for him, and live out its implications. In a real sense Jesus was something that happened in and to God for men. And the faith that men were invited to place in Jesus was not faith in a *man* who *grew* into a religious genius by religious exercises, mystical seances, ritualistic practices, or ethical activism. They were invited to place their faith in that God who clothed Himself in human flesh, and *thereby made the whole basis of man's life to be new*. It rested now with men whether they would take God's way of grace, or their own way of human "religion." Every other reading of the gospel story is a manipulation or falsification of its true thought. Any other denies the gospel and its good news.

Any anxiety as to whether or not Jesus can maintain His authority is dissipated. The authority of Jesus does not rest in His "ideals," nor in changing human philosophy, nor in scientific concepts of the nature of man and the nature of the world. It does not rest in His "ethics," nor in His world-outlook. It does not rest in His *human* genius. It is not in His "religion." It rests in God's power. And the problem as to whether we, in this century, may "diverge" from Jesus is also dissipated. Jesus is no human stereotype that we should fear to diverge from His humanness. The new Jesus is not one we imitate, else we would have to wear first-century Oriental clothes, speak Aramaic, believe the world to be flat, hold to a first-century apocalypticism, and many more things. We may diverge from Jesus in all the things that life diverges from, age to age. Jesus is different from a religious teacher, a hero, a genius. He is the eternal God-reality which becomes not an annex to our lives, but the decisive reality which becomes the center of something new and radical. He is Son of God and Saviour of the world. He comes to save us from our sins, not to teach us a new philosophy or a new "religion."

The Christ of the New Testament never argued about God or the will of God. He always confronted men with an alternative demanding decisive action. He was less an interesting teacher than an enlister, and a bringer of true life. He has nothing to say about the things of "religion." Jesus has little to say about man's religion. In fact, He is constantly attacked by proud "religious" men. Jesus exalts the man who is done with "religion," for "religion" makes man proud. He delights in the man of simple faith and obedience. He has everything to do with the realities of God and man. There was no gap between what He said and what He was. He was an activist. God confronts us directly through Him. To touch Jesus at any point is to touch the will of God. Through Him the reality of God has become flesh, as in no other way, and His statement about being one with the Father is proved by His words, which always have *power* to confront men with the righteous will and the saving love of God in human flesh. In His sense of mission He did not die as a hero; He died with the belief that through His career as a voluntary sufferer He could pierce a wall between God and man that would divide the ages and save all men. It would be eternally decisive. And that death was the very motive of His life. Through it He performed *the* divine act as by it He defeated sin and conquered death. His apocalypticism and eschatology were real, and their modern meanings are being rediscovered. True, the fanciful forms are obsolete, but the *inner meaning* is unchanged, namely, that God is Lord, and that there is a higher world which is not apprehended by thought or science, but by a faith born of obedience, penitence, and sincerity. And the "end" of history does condition all time in between the beginning and that end. The eternal meaningfulness of life, which never becomes fully manifest in a sinful world, is the real purpose of life. In that sense Jesus lived for the will of God, and in no sense was He a modern evolutionary idealist who hoped that the inner processes of nature would naturally bring about the kingdom of God. It is in that sense that His preaching must be understood. This world and God's kingdom are never identical, although the two interpenetrate. The Kingdom is final, decisive, and exists by itself.

Apocalypticism does not essentially involve the

element of fantastic catastrophe with which it has been so often associated. It is faith in the imminent relation of the real world of God's kingdom to the false present world. It speaks of the note of surprise and watchfulness which is to mark the attitude of those who know that this present world does not now manifest its true meaning. Apocalyptic faith always involves that hopeful belief in a supernatural world which is hidden in this world, which gives this world meaning, and which awaits to break forth into the world with judgment and mercy, to bring low the old order of sin, and to recreate and change the old into the new. (Jesus was hopeful, not because He thought the *world* was coming out all right; but because the *kingdom of God* was coming.) Apocalypticism feels the helplessness of human effort to correct great wrongs, and waits for God's world which is to be, to make its sovereign way into the world. It is not hopeful of the world as it is, because of any divinity of its own to lay claim upon God, but it is highly optimistic about the world that is to be because of God. This final world is to be God's world. When things look worst, then the world of God comes close to men. Then judgment and mercy meet. When they do, a new creative age comes. It might, of course, be the final end, but that is not to be our concern, for it is God's secret. We are to be faithful at our posts. Our basic faith is that God is not controlled by His creation. His kingdom *is* coming to pass. He is working and building, overruling the wrath of men for His praise. We work for the

Kingdom, because it comes. Apocalypticism believes that the world as it is has some deep, unseen meaning, and that what is happening in it has a purpose in the light of what is to be.

Eschatology is not merely interest in a final heaven. It is awareness of the final purpose and end which God is actively creating. Life and history have an "end" in view. Life must be rooted in the "end" God has in mind. As such, history and life are not fulfilled in this world. The Kingdom includes all generations. This does not stop, it intensifies social action; but it also keeps it within limits. It redeems it from sentimental utopianism as well as transcendent inactivity. Social action rooted in eschatology does not attempt the impossible in this world, nor does it rob life here of its eternal purposefulness. It rather makes life responsible always to the will of God in the present situation.

Jesus was an apocalypticist and an eschatologist. Even though we may be able to strip off much of the crass materialism, current in His day and ours, we shall never be able to escape that truth. Jesus did not possess ideas such as evolutionary progress; the infinite worth of personality; the immortality of the soul or the "persistence of personality" beyond death; the idea of the cultivation of the "inner life" as something divine; of God as an immanent integrating process in the universe; of the ethical and moral betterment of man in order to attain salvation as though it were divine merchandise. On the contrary, His whole message, because of its eschatological setting, is based upon the coming Kingdom of God, which is not man's achievement but God's gift, which judges and saves men, which demands of them a decision for or against it, and either obedience or disobedience to it. That is why Jesus Christ is the same yesterday, today and forever. He is the decisive reality of all life and of every age because in Him is the eternal truth, which is not of this changing world.

There is no *human* ideal to be found in Jesus' teaching. He gives no specific instruction as to what to do in human situations; He offers us the eternal dynamic with which to meet them. He does not think of man in his psychological phases, but of man as a unity, who must respond to God with his total being. That is why He appeals to all men, and always will appeal to them. He does not conceive of man as a being who possesses divine capacities upon which God *builds* a spiritual structure. God and man are not one, any more than any two persons are one. The kingdom of God is not a refuge, not a physical entity, nor a place of escape, but an eternal quality that holds one responsible. And that kingdom is not something universal, which Jesus helps other great men bring to light; it is a miracle of God. All men are not naturally in the Kingdom; only such as hear God's call and respond. No man has a claim upon God; God claims men! It is the coming sovereign Kingdom which gives man his individuality and not something divine which he inherently possesses. This is the distinction between Christianity

and Nazism, secular or Communist mystical naturalism. All these deny God's apartness from man.

Thus the kingdom, to Jesus, as to God, is not a
"value," not even the highest value of man. God
and kingdom are not the *"ends"* of *man's* existence:
they are *beginnings* of divine activity for and in men.
The parables of the seed and the leaven do not convey the idea of evolutionary progress, but only the
idea of the sudden, the miraculous, the great, pro-
ceeding from the insignificant.

This meaning of eschatology is woven into the
warp and woof of Jesus' teaching. Nothing less than
the idea of the kingdom as essentially superhistorical
is involved. Men are invited to enter into it, but
they cannot build it. It comes to them. It is not an
ideal end of human history. It is the sovereignty of
God. And to a sovereign God there is no such thing
as progress. When He speaks, all life stands still.

Jesus is not to be merely imitated by those who
think they can approximate Him; He is to be devo-
tionally believed, followed, and appropriated by those
who feel their distance from Him, as well as His
condescending power to lift them to possess their
divine sonships with a self-giving God. True Christian life comes not of ethical straining after perfection, but of living faith in the grace of God that is
born of penitence.

Jesus did not instruct men about the God within
them, so much as He radiated in unmistakable fashion the sovereign power of an objective God. No
one, He remarks, enters the realm of God, or knows

God, by being clever, or rich, or ethical, or "religious." One knows God by a special decision of faith that involves the whole man. To get into the kingdom one does not intensify his humanity; one surrenders the human will.

Therefore, Paul did not repeat the words of Jesus. He was not much concerned about the man Jesus. He was far more concerned with the Christ of decisive power who gave to men an inward drive of life that impelled them to organize their thoughts around a new focus. Paul, and New-Testament Christians, got something from Christ which was not human and which they could not get anywhere else. Jesus is not a static dispenser of ethical or philosophical "principles," but a generator of new humanity sensitized by life's divine Lord.

Those who hope to cull out of the Gospels an "ethic of Jesus" are of all people most miserable, for Jesus gave no detailed ethics, in a technical sense. His high demands are such that they can never be put into actual practice. They are meant to confront men with decision for the absolute. They furnish the basis for a constantly sensitized conscience born of repentance for sin, with which Christians meet every life-situation, and which makes Christian ethics a living, growing, personal responsibility and relationship with God and man. As remarked above, Jesus has little to do with "religion." He is "the *conqueror*," not the fighter. "He is the herald of the divine will, the champion of the divine honor, the authoritative bearer of divine power. . . . The significance of

His life lies in its possessing an actuality which no religion possesses—the actuality of the unapproachable, the incomprehensible, the inconceivable—the realization of that possibility which passes human consideration, 'Behold, I make all things new.'" He *has* overcome the world.

This is what Karl Barth has called the "vehemence of his consciousness." In Jesus, Truth is no longer distant, reserved, and transcendent in its attitude toward reality. In Him the two—reality and truth—are one. He brings with Him the power to make God concrete in human situations. He makes redemption an activity within human flesh. He gives all that is human its true meaning, and He interprets God and man to one another.

That is why He calls men *to* Him, He challenges men to a *decision*, He speaks in paradoxical terms demanding a radical change in the minds of people who would follow Him. He has to do with the absolutely *last* question and answer of life, which reside in every moment of life, and not with expedient measures of the present. Therefore He says that a camel cannot get through a needle's eye, and that one must sell all to get into the Kingdom, of which He is the herald. His kingdom world is beyond, yet qualifyingly in, this world. The impossibility of the Kingdom in this world throws those who sense it back upon God. Great social reformers have always been deeply spiritual. Jesus has the power to transcend the centuries, confronting whom, men of every age feel as though time had ceased to be. He is the eternal Reality itself, and as such meets man at the spot where man can truly see himself as the sinner he is and as the child of God he is called to be.

The Gospels are, therefore, not really "biographies" of Jesus; they are flaming witnesses of His glory and His power. They tell us none of the things that we highly prize in other religious biographies. There is no glorifying of His human capacities, in the hope that a glorified or divinely energized *human* capacity might become God. Man does not thus give birth to God. In the lowliness of human faith and obedience God *is born* of Himself within men where men let Him be God.

Far from being a hero, Jesus is humble before God. His glory is hidden from public view. The revelation of the glory of God in Jesus is not a miraculous theophany, but one that must be seen in its lowliness. For God will not have Himself to be known in something freakish. And Jesus dies, obedient unto death, for in His very defeat (so unlike idealism) the voice of God speaks clearest. That is why the cross best reveals God. God wants our trusting faith and not our applause. A revelation great in outward appearance would soon be developed into an idolatry. It would not turn us to God *in faith*. Jesus must be followed in faith and trust, not exalted in pageant and image. His deity is not outwardly manifest. It is discerned only by those penitents who see beyond the veil of the humility of Jesus.

The real Christ cannot be called "historical" at all.

Who can write the life of that Something that arrested and changed early Christians? Who can cross the boundary and enter into the holy of holies of His real secret essence? It is this Christ we are seeing again today. He is One who smashes all our illusions concerning our own goodness, who will not let us tack Him onto, or use Him for, our religious or intellectual or social schemes. He will not let us resolve Him into a stereotype, or a "religious Man," or make an ethical set of principles out of His teachings. He is the Word, and as such He is the divine authority. He bombards the inner citadel of our proud life; He tears the shams off our social order and our churches. He attacks our total self. He will not allow Himself to be made into a system of any kind whereby we may enhance ourselves. He will be Lord or nothing. He is no founder of an "ism." He is the Reality of God as it confronts men in every age, along life's highways, in the flesh, everywhere. For this "new" Jesus is not less, but more, human. About the time men think they have Him explained as a liberal genius of religious prophecy, or as a static dispenser of orthodox creeds and codes, He has a way of loosing Himself from their graveclothes and going on before, or of entering into their counsels through locked doors.

Today the Church should not apologize for this Christ, nor seek to "explain" Him, but should proclaim His reality fearlessly as the One without whom we shall be lost. In none other is there salvation. There is no other Way.

A modern Christian thinker has said that with the high conception of Jesus held by our fathers something could be done, because it was like a rushing torrent coming from a mountain glacier, while the low conception of Jesus that is held by some today is like a stagnant pool which man hopelessly attempts to force to the heights by a hand pump.

Jesus Christ is the pledge of God that He is still God, and that He is minded in love and judgment toward the children of men. Therefore Jesus Christ is man's hope, his forgiveness, his reason for living, his assurance of God's rightness and victory. One great Christian, who was a monotheist, said that for him to live was Christ! That is an audacious thing for a mortal man to say. Yet it is man's highest confession and his most blessed hope. To see in Jesus Christ the good will of God manifested in spite of all things that point to the contrary, is to have an anchorage and a dynamic for living that cannot be surpassed in mortal history. No human philosophy has that power. This Christ is God's Word to despairing and seeking man, to assure him that God *is* still God and that in His own good time He is bringing all things to His own fulfillment and fruition. Through this Christ God does not condemn us, but He does humble our pride, and thereby seek to enlist us in the only cause that can eventually redeem the world.

Christ is God's Way, God's Truth, God's Light, God's Life, God's leaven, God's power, God's atoning love among men, given out of sheer love and offered to us all without money or price. It is for our salvation, our enjoyment, our blessedness. It is for the whole world, and therefore is not to be proudly hoarded by saint or Church. And no man has a right to condition that free gift of God by any relative organization or human authority, lest God's Christ be made less than *God's* gift for all men.

With such a Christ, it is impossible to be overcome of the world. For He *is* the victory of God and no man can or dare make Him less, or seek, by his own means, to effect so perfect a way of salvation as that which God alone could and did give.

"*I came* that ye might *have life! I am the vine.* Without me ye can do nothing. *I am* the light of the world, and he that walketh in the light does not stumble in the darkness.*"* There is *none* other name given among men whereby they might be saved! None other but the name of Jesus Christ, who is nothing less than the living God in human flesh, revealing Himself as Lord of life and of history. For Jesus Christ means the Lordship of God dwelling among men. He needs no defense, only faithful trust and joyous walking and willing service and perfect confidence in the way He has appointed, apart from which all ways are the ways of erring man.

Jesus Christ, the same yesterday, today, and forever! Why? Because the real quality in Him is eternal God, beyond which there is nothing else or more. Rejoice, and again I say, *rejoice!* Emmanuel! O come, let us worship, let us bow down, let us kneel!

CHAPTER IX

THE CHRISTIAN MESSAGE

THERE might be much confusion in any Christian group should its leadership be called upon to declare what really is the Christian message. The answer today dare not be provincial, nor can it be denominational. Nor dare it be the answer of a professional unionist, who likewise has his idea as to what the Christian message is. The answer must be nothing less than a penitent and humble confession of *the Christian Message*. Such a Christian message can best be summed up in two words—Jesus Christ. "Jesus Christ" is two words, and each one means a reality. We will need to search not only the Scriptures but the whole of our Christian tradition and history to ascertain in all fullness just what is the length and the breadth and the height of that which is in Christ Jesus. But our discovery will be nothing less or more than Jesus Christ.

Human beings have but one fundamental question to ask. It is necessary that it be answered. And men must answer it for themselves, consciously or unconsciously, or they could not keep on living. It is the question about life, its meaning, destiny, and goal. They want to know if there is a personal God; if He cares; if He has spoken to them, and if He has done anything for them. They want to know the why, the what, the wherefore, and the whence of existence.

Human existence carries within itself this disturbing question about life and God.

We are surrounded with no positive and conclusive evidences about the nature of God. In truth He is "unknown" and hidden. We have many fragmentary hints as to His existence, but we are restless until we *know* the Unknown. It is this human drive that gives man his unique personal nature, in spite of his sin, and puts him above the brutes. When a man recognizes this dualism—this basic drive toward God in the light of that basic egotistical drag which clings to his vital, earthly existence, then he becomes desperate about a message, about finding the answer to the riddle of his existence. He wants to know if God has answered his quest. Upon this the message of Christianity must rest, to it it must appeal, and upon it it must build. The missionary activity of historic Christianity was possible because of this fundamental universal human drive and the God-initiated gospel's satisfaction of that need.

Early Protestantism grew out of this moral riddle of life. It is epitomized in Luther's early years. He was a true human being in his desperate search for freedom from the drag and enslavement of evil which caused his enlightened conscience to accuse him of guilt. He was seeking salvation and could not save himself from his sin. He was not an intellectual attempting a rational or theological synthesis, nor a reconciliation of science and religion, nor of philosophy with Christianity. He was seeking to reconcile his will to God's will, his deepest ethical and personal self to God, for that was his first, last, and inescapable problem. Luther had sensed that life's riddle is essentially moral and existential, not intellectual or theoretical. He saw the crisis of man and God.

In following with ascetic rigidity the prescribed method for obtaining salvation, Luther worked havoc with his health. The more human ethical deeds he performed, the more his personality seemed to disintegrate. His pride grew thereby. An attempted escape into the higher realm of Christian ideals helped him not at all; it never got him beyond his problem. He did not get beyond his human possibility, and religiously, salvation must be powerful enough to root life in something beyond the human present possibility. Human intensification is not Christian salvation.

Psychologists have sought to account for Luther's "morbidity" in his student carousals, his questionable thoughts of sex, and a sensitive conscience which suffered from the stern medieval education of prudish parents. Catholic scholars have called his whole moral life in question. But these criticisms do not escape the minimum problem, which was not peculiarly Luther's, but which is the problem of every human being when he is face to face with the evil burden of life; when he is earnestly seeking God. A mere message of morality will not suffice. Logic will not do! Theosophical principles, idealistic philosophy, mysticism fail, for an invitation to enter the fool's paradise of monistic idealism only alleviates the problem for the present; it will return with seven more devils when another crisis appears. Reality, not ideals, not programs, not self-hypnosis, will do! Failure to see the problem, ignorance of it, or a deliberate attempt to rationalize it, will inevitably lead to a weak illusory solution, which only aggravates the case when the crisis comes. Failure to answer the problem will lead to a vitiating skepticism which levels life to the plane of the animal and in time dissolves the very essence of personality. Luther arrived at the conviction that his chief difficulty in solving his problem as regards God was moral guilt. Something inherent in his very soul blocked the way, and no moral deed could surmount it. His essential evil self, with its ungodly ego, seemed enhanced, rather than decreased, by the merits of rigid moral endeavor. He could not save himself, he could not get to God by striving alone.

It was then that he was led, through a period of study, to read the New Testament, especially the letter to the Galatians. Here he found *the* message that has become the cornerstone of Protestantism: You are saved by *grace* through *faith*. Not by works, not by human effort or merit, not by any human institution or creed, but through the sheer goodness of a *sovereign God*, by an *act* of His which has removed the contradiction of life, and pledged the love of God, which is apprehended and appropriated through the receptacle of trusting faith. Luther's discovery was a rediscovery of the original gospel. God has *come* to men. The original *naïve* message which

Protestantism rediscovered was the message of the sovereignty of God and His love, His grace and His righteousness. Apart from any human formulae or power, God works through, yet independently of, them. All human factors are but means, receptacles in which the Word of God is contained and conveyed and preserved, but the receptacle is not the Word itself. Not even the Bible *is* the Word of God. It may be loosely said to be, but upon careful definition it must not be identified with the Word. As Zwingli said, the Word is the pith, the sense, the root of the spirit *in* the external words. What Luther discovered, and what Protestantism has lived on in subsequent centuries, was the gospel of grace which Paul possessed, and which he proclaimed against the materialistic Judaizers of his day who had imprisoned God within human legalisms and institutions. For Paul, as for Luther, *God alone* confronts the human soul in His sovereign character through the historic Jesus in a once-for-all divine deed. *God came to man!* God is *a priori* and never *a posteriori*. That was the essential, free, spiritual religion of God.

This discovery of Luther's worked havoc with the Church, for men had access to the grace of God irrespective of ecclesiastical mediation. It worked havoc with the intellectual structure of scholasticism. It worked havoc with the penitential system. Salvation was free, and was based upon the only sovereign—God.

This was Protestantism's original, liberating message. This is still its unitive gospel. This reconciliation between man and God has issued from the merciful initiative of God. Its attainment was humanly impossible. The primary meaning of repentance is a frank acknowledgment that we cannot create or control the gospel of God. It involves self-negation and crucifixion of the evil, self-centered, "old man." Christ is the Reconciliator, the Mediator, not merely a genius or a pioneer in goodness. He reveals the ungodly evil tendencies of human existence, because He mirrors our eternal hope in the divine existence. The forgiveness of sin must issue from Christ or the evil offense resident within human nature will not be removed. Christ is *the* Way, *the* Truth, and, above all, *the* Life—He is both dynamic and eschatological hope.

Early Protestantism insisted as the focal message of its genius that God offers the initiative; that He offers the reconciliation, the atonement; that He alone answers man's deepest problem; and that righteousness is not attained by a humanistic working out, under direction, of what would be humanly possible, but is freely granted by an objective act of God's self-giving love. All philosophies fail here, for none of them knows a God who acts and moves. Religions fail for the same reason, with the exception of Judaism in its highest prophetic utterances (but they are rare and undiscovered without the fuller interpretation of Christ). For religions are, after all, only human *strivings* after God. Jesus Christ is God's *act* in coming to men. Therein lies the difference between religion and faith in the Christian sense.

Faith, which apprehends God, is essentially an act of the whole person, prompted by the seeking Shepherd's footsteps within the deep realm of the God-given, but perverted, conscience. Faith is repentant trust in a person, and not mere intellectual assent, or active, imitative, ethical following. Men imagine that this emphasis might work toward a moral laxity in the believer, since his salvation depends upon a message and an act of God rather than upon man's ethical and intellectual endeavors. But quite to the contrary, history proves that the greatest social and missionary effects have resulted from God-invaded humans who sought only to return, in a spirit of thanksgiving for their redemption, some "millionth part" of their debt. The most radical and reckless ethics have been practiced not by ethicists, nor philosophers, nor scientists, but by those born of a critical religious redemption. The savoring salt must have saltiness, the illuminating light must have the essence of light. Christian ethics issue from the Christian man of faith.

It requires no strain to see the change that has come in Protestantism's message during the years. The sense of sin as an inherent perversity involving all men in guilt, is quite out of date. The human may commit sins, but he is not *sinful*. There is less interest in that divine wrath and that hatred of inherent sin which burden men's lives, and which lie at the basis of this lost world. The dualistic ethical basis of Christianity has been largely dissolved.

Some have even suggested that the sense of sin is due to a reprehensible education. Rid the race of that sense of sin, it has been said, and it will progress indefinitely. Sin has been made a trifling thing which bears no direct relation to God, which the Bible repeatedly affirms it does. It has become a mere external offense against the body. Sin does not make God "unknown" through its pernicious character in the mind of modern man. In consists of violations of the social contract, or ecclesiastical *mores*. Jesus' insistence that the inner sins of attitude—indifference, pharisaism, and the like—are the worst, is minimized. The absolute standard of Jesus is eliminated or toned down. Psychical experts hope to bring up spectral ghosts out of the subconscious, believing that the sunlight of a light-hearted laugh might put them to flight! The forgiveness of sin has been dropped from the lists of sermon topics, because it is unpopular, or no longer means much to the modern congregation, or to the minister. Sermons on the atonement are studied affairs, in the hope that they may be adjusted to modern thought. The atonement has been made quite a natural affair of personality adjustment. The cross is magnified as the heroic "last stand" of a religious genius for His ideals. As such it is colored with the deification of man. It becomes then a part of the natural incarnation of God immanently in His creation. Then Jesus *becomes* a divine Leader by His death. The fact that its necessity was a terrible life-burden which brought forth bloody perspiration and the terrible cross has been delicately made an aside. The cross suffers today from a superficial interpretation. To say it was merely the "last stand" of a Hero for His ideals is to violate its real meaning according to the New-Testament writers. The cross means judgment. It means sovereign, once-for-all forgiveness. It is that about Jesus which cuts counter to the *status quo* of that age and all ages. It was dreaded by Jesus all through His life. Not only did He fear the dread defilement of death, which was strong in His Hebrew mind, but He feared the real sting of death, which was never physical pain, but moral evil, forsakenness of God. Death, to Jesus, was linked up with the lost world, it was the last victorious stab of the Prince of Evil. Jesus always faced the cross as One who really understood the terror of death, which was sin and not mere animal fright or any *mysterium tremendum.*

In the New-Testament faith the cross is not so much the length to which one would go in attaining the highest reaches of human perfection. True, that meaning may be read into the significance of the cross. But in a more natural interpretation and less artificial sense, the cross, to the early Christian, was the marvelous reach of divine love to the lowest depths of human sin and need. The whole gospel story as recorded, even in the Synoptics, offers very little for the human being to boast about. The Gospels do not give us primarily the human story of Jesus in His search for, and His discovery of, God. Rather, it is the divine story of God's life in Jesus, showing God's search for, and discovery of, man in his blindness, ignorance, lameness, imprisonment, and state of relativity and sin! That is the background of the gospel story, and it is indeed far from the present popular notion of the life and the message of Jesus.

The modern tendency to tone down sin is due not so largely to more enlightenment of the mind as to the brazenness of a superficial self-sufficiency that refuses to look death and raw human life calmly in the face and see their demoniac reality. It is this omnipotent humanism that fails to understand that the last and most important week of Jesus' life occupies more space, in proportion, than any other period of His life. The message of Christianity will suffer so long as men look at themselves through colored spectacles in a trick mirror. The early Church made the forgiveness of sins, pledged through the love of God evidenced in the crucified *Jesus*, one of the pillars of their simple faith. "I delivered unto you *first*, . . . Christ died for our sins."

A decline in the doctrine of the wrath of God naturally involves a loss of the idea of God's sovereign righteousness in history and the necessity of the ancient equivalent of hell, real, if not permanent. Variations in the natural order, when contrary to law, involve intense suffering. But in the higher world of spirituality we think it does not operate. God is made into a salubrious Grandfather who condones our innocent follies upon a mere expression on our part that we intend to reform. The idea of a loving

Father who shoulders man's sins, who is tragically wounded for man's iniquities, who desires our healing through His own stripes, who in unbelievable love accepts the burden that was ours, is not understood today. It is pretty poetry to those who do not understand the A B C of evil's reality.

No one of us could accept a medieval God, who with the glaring eyes of an arbitrary wrath watches every act of misconduct. But that God is righteous is an affirmation of the conscience and the soul crushed with the burden of this world's unrighteousness. God is not "soft mush." If He had no reaction to evil, we could not respect Him. The inner depths of the soul cry out for the living God, knowing instinctively that this world is not a world in which God is Lord. That hell exists is a fact anyone can observe if he ventures beyond the walls of his sheltered cloister into the highways of human existence. Anyone who really knows his own life knows hell. An inflexible Will works against the background of things. What a man sows he reaps. Even divine forgiveness cannot stop the ax as it falls at the root of men and nations. Laws of nature operate in the opposite direction too when man injects his ungodly will into their processes. But that does not make God evil. His mercy is always beyond His justice!

None the less, hell is still a reality, more terrible than ever. Loss of ethical distinctions, the fixation of "great gulfs" of self-interested character, the subtle undermining of the whole social structure of truth and honesty, the impotence of constant, gnawing and inner friction, the undying flame of a turbulent con-science; yes, and, finally, disintegration of personal-ity—these and their universal physical expressions in social and individual life are facts.

The present situation in the economic world and in society in general, is a mute, yet unmistakable, wit-ness to the fact that sowing to the wind will reap the whirlwind, and that a Babel-building civilization, which forgets God as it deals with men and things which He created, will crash, and sooner or later will have to do with demons. God is not mocked! His-tory is strewn with the "wrecks of empires," because they magnified the relative into the absolute. When men forget "the earth is the Lord's and the fullness thereof," and appropriate these for their *own* ends, they are in for ruin. The love of God is wonderful, but it is a strong, upright, and manly love, unlike the sentimentality preached by us moderns, or the controlled systematic love of the orthodox. It is sovereign, free, living, and unconditioned.

The joy of salvation too has passed as a character-istic of the modern Christian. To hear Kagawa speak of Christian joy is to know how blessed it is. Many have known that blessed feeling in the knowl-edge of redemption from the guilt and bondage of damning evil. It resulted in ethical thankfulness. It expressed itself in song. A Paul could rejoice within prison walls. Persecution and hardships could not stifle it. For chained in "prisons dark, they were still in heart and conscience free." How can there be joy in a religion that has lost its motive, its lofty basis, and its marvelous God-initiated redemption? The scientific laboratories, and the schools of ethics and philosophy know no hymns. Theories of the universe, of ethics, and the hypotheses of experimenters play no organs. When the inaccessible world of God goes from human aspiration, the gospel goes too! Poetry becomes prose, and heaven becomes earth.

Many services of worship are devoid of worship. Often the sermons appeal to the mind, in the hope that Christianity might be intellectually respectable. Or they essay upon some moralism, inviting man to struggle through as best he can, for "to be a Christian is to be a *man* at *his best!*" Or they learnedly descant upon some phase of the psychology of religion; exhort upon some program for the preservation of the ecclesiastical organization.

Topical sermons abound. Little is made of the objective facts upon which the Christian religion is based. These are usually utilized to shed light upon our subjective experience, instead of being regarded as sovereign norms to which we must adjust ourselves. Little wonder that prayer is a problem—and worship self-glorification. Hymns abound in the first personal pronoun. The preacher becomes an interpreter of events in the terms of general religious ideals. He loses his prophetic function of proclaiming the eternal gospel of God. He becomes a mere servant of men. As a result his message is shorn of divine authority and audacity. He takes his place in the ranks of other cultural connoisseurs of his

age. This is exceedingly dangerous business, for it
may rob the Christian minister of his justification for
his existence.   There should be something which,
regardless of men's opinions, a minister *must* do and
say.   The Catholic clergyman holds his office not at
the permission of men, but at the command of God,
and he must celebrate the sacrament of the mass,
whether he cares to or not, and whether people are
present or not. If the Protestant clergyman has no
similar sacrament of the Word, the Message, why is
he a minister?

When religion is made to originate, not in God,
but in the consciousness of man, the result for the
Protestant message is axiomatic.   Christianity becomes a social technique.   It may become a science-
religion synthesis, an ethical theism, a mystic pantheism, or a technique for "personal expression."
It may aspire to the heights of a synthetic sociology
that reaches into the realms of a universal eclecticism.
It may become a functional adjunct to culture, a program for "social Christianization," a technique of
race melioration.   Christianity certainly has its personal and social effects in these branches of society,
but these are not its main concern. These are *results*
and *external* effects of the essence of Christianity,
which is directed toward units and not groups, toward
the conscience and not the mind, toward the produc-
tion of faith and not mental consistency.

Christianity's original message is not grounded in
any human formula or understanding of God, but in
God alone.   Its content is not dependent purely upon

intellectual comprehension, subject to the changing ages of men. Nor is its content a mere ethical code, whether individual or social. Nor is it an orthodox emotional reaction. It has nothing to do with baptisms, orders, politics, economic theories, social systems, as such. It rests upon the existential, ethical nature of God and of man, of all ages, colors, climes, and classes. It is not concerned with the peripheral thought-forms, cultures, or languages of men. It is a message meant for the citadel of the ego in man.

This message demands an either-or decision. Argument is unnecessary. Its demand strikes deeper than the intellect. Its validity is not in the experience of its recipient, but in its Subject. Truth is sovereign. It verifies itself, and does not depend on any human apologetic to substantiate it. That is why God's Word, His message, cannot be defended with intellectual formulae. It must be witnessed to, preached, and testified about. Its messenger must be a "crier," an ambassador, a preacher—his message is a *kerugma*. It is not *of* men, although it comes *through* men; it is *of* God. It does not depend upon men for its authority. This message is first, the hearer second. And that Word strikes through human differences, and appeals to all men in the recesses of their inmost souls, in their consciences, demanding faith and absolute surrender.

Faith; a trustful, recipient mood receives it. Faith is the childlike spirit, the humble, teachable, attentive attitude of listening to authority. In that respect even Abraham becomes a Christian. By faith we let

God be both Judge and Redeemer. By faith we give up our own rightness. Luther said that Adam was the first Christian. This attitude of faith runs throughout the Scriptures. The small and insignificant things confound the wise. The needy person with a sense of dependence represents the true attitude of man over against this message of God. Faith is not passivity; it is an active participation in the ethical walk demanded by the message. It results in turning away from a life dedicated to the self, to a life dedicated to God.

This message of Christianity, which is the Word of God, demands critical decision. The Word is bigger than the words of the Bible. It is primarily an act. It brooks no other loyalty. It has, however, no absolute dogmatic assurance to offer the recipient —only such as can be had of God in a changing world of time. It demands constant vigilance, repentance, struggle, and prayerful expectation. At best our theologies are relative "interim theologies." But this faith, though it cannot be proved, demands constant following, and in that following, it substantiates itself to the believer, through the work of the Holy Spirit. Faith is as miraculous as the resurrection and the incarnation. It is not a human event in the fullest sense. We can never exhaustively possess in earthly vessels the property of God's world. But we do possess it in a fashion, *but only* in faith, and faith is living trust.

This brings us to the complementary doctrine of Protestantism, which parallels that of God's sovereignty working through His grace and His love and His righteousness. The counterpart of that message, in human terms, is repentance. Repentance has been thought of as weakness. It was associated with the repentance of monks who retired to monasteries and in Buddhistic fashion sought to eradicate normal human desires. It was also associated with the extravagant emotionalism of the revival, with its extreme suggestion of the masses, which robbed one of individuality and made him hysterical. Such repentance is not repentance in the New-Testament sense, any more than is the remorse of those who have committed grievous physical sins.

Repentance was preached by Jesus continually. Every contact He made with men shows that He demanded a repentant spirit. From His first manifesto—"Repent ye, for the kingdom of heaven is at hand"—to His last conversation with the condemned thief, His spirit rejoiced at the presence of repentance in a human soul.

Repentance is the attitude of moral and religious receptivity. It is self-crucifixion. It is the spirit of expectant waiting, of obedient trust, of faithful following. Repentance is spiritual adjustment to the world of God. It is the seeking attitude, the spirit of the inquirer, the knocker, the prayer, the drinker, the eater. It is the spirit of willing absorption. A repentant person is not a weakling. In fact, he is showing the strongest creative quality that human beings possess. Though it may seem to be an emptying of all his human personality, in reality repentance is the reception into life of all that God gives. It means acknowledging that we are God's and that we belong to Him, and that only as His possession do we become the creatures we ought to be. To be repentant means that one puts himself into the attitude whereby he most efficiently channels the power of the unconditioned Kingdom. It signifies that life has been made a vessel and not a content.

In the social sense, repentance is the acknowledgment that we have need of each other, and that we cannot live the selfish life of aloof individualism. Jesus offers us the best illustration of social repentance in His baptism, which was not a manifesto of His personal sin. Rather, it was the frank identification of Himself with the sins of mankind, the feeling that wherever the effects of unbrotherliness were felt, He was involved. That is repentance.

In the intellectual sense, repentance is the constant willingness to rethink our basic convictions, always realizing that our dogmas and our creeds are but relative expressions of a constant and abiding Reality. It is the willingness to learn, to seek, to ask, and to pray. It is the embodiment of the spirit that one has need always to take heed lest he fall. "There is but One who is Good." *We* are liable to err. We possess only tentative knowledge. We are creatures and not the Creator!

Repentance involves not only those who have committed grievous physical sins, but all men. Jesus frankly taught that the worst sins are not those external violations of the ecclesiastical code, but those inner attitudes of pride, self-esteem, and, above all, of self-sufficient moral conceit. All have come short of the glory of God, all have sinned and are sinners. We *are* sin! Therefore salvation from God is a gift, and as such no one has a right to boast about it. The common acknowledgment of our common receptivity of God's gift makes us brothers in His grace. While Jesus never condoned the crass sins of the flesh, He nevertheless expressed Himself most vehemently against the current idea that they were the only sins for which a man should repent. To Jesus, repentance was demanded of all men, regardless of their station or moral cleanliness. Jesus' demands were severest upon moral perfectionists.

For this reason, original Protestantism made much of grace. We are saved by grace! It was a rediscovery of the spiritual and free religion of Paul— and of Jesus. Grace was the active, present good will of God, which had always been in force, even in Old-Testament times, and which had been pledged to men in a most evident manner in Jesus of Nazareth. Alas, Protestantism soon turned away from this revolutionary discovery, and again involved the free religion of God in ecclesiastical camps and theological parties. Jesus was again made the Founder of a particular Church, of a particular dogma or system, instead of the Founder of *the* religion of God and *the* religion of man. Man wanted a religion of his own; he was not content with the Father's house. Repentance was violated by being forced into human molds of definition. Repentance no longer meant childlike faith in a free and sovereign God who saves by grace.

The modern decline of real repentance in the Church has been due to the same old human sin. Man attempts to control God by his human capacities and seeks to judge and control men for his own ends. He seeks always to dissolve the dualism between himself and his Creator, and to dissolve his unity with his brothers. He refuses to admit that there is a sovereign God over whom he has no control, to whom he is responsible and debtor, and by whose hand he is saved. In recent years man has thought that his mind could explain everything, and that his scientific genius could control everything, and God was relegated to those realms where His mind and His science did not yet obtain as master. Man utilized everything to his own advantage, whether it was his fellow man or his crops or the minerals in the soil. He never gave much thought to the question, "Whose are these things I handle?"

Man transcendentalized his powers. Success became his heaven, and self-aggression his religion. Gold became his Lord. The West with its marvelous daily conveniences was thought to be the kingdom of heaven, and some Christian missionaries thought of evangelism in terms of bringing scientific benefits to the heathen. Jesus in a sack suit was the successful go-getter, the Man who could handle men. But of repentance, that prime authority and demand of men? All talk about sin was thought of as a reversal to the abnormal. Psychology had taught men to forget the idea. On the contrary, human motives were essentially good, and with a little education the saint would be forthcoming. But repentance? Even the churches imbibed the idea of self-assertion and activity. They thought of the successful church and minister in terms of physical activity. The church became a social club with a calendar bulging with conflicting dates. But of repentance? That beautiful spirit of dependence, which should be the chief characteristic of every church that seeks to be a fellowship of Jesus, was discredited. The Church, of all institutions, should house the front line of God's emergence into the world. Of all places, the Church is the one in which the conditions for God's coming are ripe. She is His bride and the mother of His sons. But a worldly Church that has lost its prime characteristic hazards not only its future, its present justification, but the life of the moral and social world as well.

A world that has been allowed to go on and on in the spirit of selfish aggressiveness, without the check of continual warning by a true Church, is bound to suffer the inevitable result of its excessive unrepentance. When any age forgets that the capacities of men, the minerals in the soil, the life of the brother man, are not man's to hold and to use for his own ends, then its decay is inevitable. When men seek to be masters, controllers, Gods—instead of repentant brothers, creatures, receivers, sinners—they will reap what they sow with the same inevitability as harvest follows seedtime.

The Church must again become the prophetic mouthpiece of God, preaching repentance in the spirit of repentance as never before. People may be baffled by a message so contrary to the trends of the age. But they need to be told the truth—to repent. And to repent means to have done with every illusion, to repent of their "religious" ideas of God, to acknowledge that there is but *one* way out, and that that is God's way. It means to acknowledge with sincerity and honesty that in our impossibility there is One Great Possibility—God. In our Calvary, both of Church and social order, there is One Easter. In our valley of death there is but One Life. In our doubt there is but One Affirmation. The refreshment of God is not withheld from us because of God's unwillingness to give. It is not ours because we do not sincerely repent. We will not *admit* we need God. Therein is our sin. The Kingdom is at hand! The kingdom of God is within you—even though it is *not you.* God wants to *happen* to men and the world. The Vision Glorious of far-off horizons wants to break in upon man's dark world. Repent! Admit it! You cannot deny its existence, nor can you prove its being, or deny its right. There *is* a dualism between God and men. God wants to unite it. Repent!

This is Christianity's greatest doctrine. It must repossess it with a great conviction. Evangelical Protestantism, which has done so much to stimulate the individualism of the West, needs to revive the counter doctrine of repentance. Protestantism,

which has unduly bolstered up the idea of thrift, and
with it of capitalistic enterprise, needs to preach with
greater vigor than ever before the repentant attitude
of the comradeship of men in the fabric of guilt, as
well as of salvation. The social side of salvation is
not one apart. It is but another side of the individual gospel.

The message of the New Testament was simple.
Nowhere can we better discover the essential unitive message of decisive Christianity than in the missionary messages of Paul. He was no apologist for
a philosophy or an ethic, but a witness to a deep conviction born of faith. Jesus "announced" even as
He taught.

These missionary messages were usually addressed
to Israelites, and from that basis as an apperceptive
point of contact they preached Christ. But when
they announced the Kingdom message to the Greeks,
they proceeded according to a different method.
They interpreted to the Gentiles a hidden world,
latent within, which spoke of God, but which they
had not sufficiently grasped to properly articulate.
For the God-idea is common to all men; it is the
basis of all religion. There is no people in whom
there has not been discovered some trace of a God-
consciousness, working itself out in rituals, religious
customs, and taboos. But always these speak of a
hidden unknown God whom men ignorantly worship. Jesus is not immediately brought into the picture. He is later set into that universal framework
as the focal personal interpreter of all things. For

after this general knowledge is preached, without arousing particular dissatisfaction, the more specific knowledge is presented: "And the times of this ignorance God winked at; but now commandeth all men everywhere to repent; because he hath appointed a day, in the which he will judge the world in righteousness by that man whom he hath ordained; whereof he hath given assurance unto all men, in that he hath raised him from the dead." This declaration of a Day of Judgment, and the end of Time-process; this demand for ethical repentance; this setting of Jesus Christ to be the final Arbiter of destiny, raised from the dead and the "first fruits of them that slept"—all this is unique and decisive. This qualifies and characterizes the general knowledge which men possess of God's Creatorhood. It is this personal and ethical note that divides men, wherever Christ is preached. Some mock, some desire another hearing, some accept.

The New Testament is filled with this message. There shall be an end to Time, and all things are gradually growing toward that climax. In spite of all we may say about Paul's Greek background, the fact remains that he stoutly maintained this concept of the "end." He is no exclusive Platonist hoping for the evolution of the world into the higher realm of the Time-world, nor is he exclusively a pessimistic Buddhist, hoping for the total extinction of all desires in Nirvana. *God* alone is the world's hope.

This pure, *naïve*, universal wistfulness about God, which all men possess, has been vitiated by a creature-worship. The witness of God's righteousness, which is the possession of every mortal with any degree of moral and religious sincerity in the face of life's supreme question, has been blinded by a worship of self. The whole race is corporately involved in this "Titanism." That is why the *whole* race must stand judgment before God. Not individual trespasses, but *racial apostasy* is meant, which confuses God with things He created. Sin has but one root. All sins are but branches of this trunk. It is ingrained in man's very nature, and it is social. This tendency of man to worship himself is the scarlet thread that binds the history of the world together in a fabric of sin. Selfish individualism and practical atheism are man's chief sin. And it is for this reason that men have lost their fulcrum of life, and, with it, their true standards. All men, in varying degrees, are unbalanced in judgments, insights, and viewpoints. Every vice, from the pharisaism of the elite to the viciousness of low passions—yes, and to the religious self-hypnotism of the mystic—is basically rooted in this arch sin of self-worship. Physical sufferings the world over are its effects. International unrest, armaments, wars, slavery, and death are its direct consequences. Death is not merely physical; it is an indication of an inner, essential, fatal, disintegrating malady. The loss of the sense of God, which always accompanies the rise of material civilizations and of the spirit of man, is the substratum of our spiritual insanity.

Since this is the problem which confronts the

world, the important question is, Is there a way out
of our guilt, a possibility that defies the present impossibility? Upon this question the early Christian
message was specific. Not that the fine speculations
found in Paul were presented to Gentiles, who would
never have understood the Hebrew *Weltanschauung*.
But Christianity *has* a message to the world which
man loses in his conceit. The message centered in a
Man whom God had appointed to be Judge of the
entire world. He "places" them and is the ground
of their destinies. Not that destiny is determined by
man's comprehension or intellectual grasp of Jesus
Christ. He comprehends and grasps men. Since it
is God who judges through this Man, is there a
single man who can escape Him? He also offers
forgiveness and pardon and life eternal—directly!
And this judgment and pardon is not only in the
future. He has already come into the world and is
continually judging and pardoning it. And this Man
is not a mere teacher, for as such He has no redemp-
tive mission. His is not only a mission of teaching
what is latent within us. He is *the* Word of God,
the Message. He is the pledge of God's forgiveness
and love, of God's resurrection and power over the
world. This is the chief characteristic of Christianity. Jesus Christ is no mere human ethical ideal, He
is Saviour, He is *the* Logos. He *was* Immanuel!
Jesus Christ is not one among other Saviours of the
world. He is not even the highest ideal of human
thought. He is not even to be "valued" as God.
That would still make Him earthly, from beneath.

He is neither *a* door, nor *a* way, nor *a* truth. He is
in reality *the* Way, *the* Truth, and *the* Life. There
is no way to the Father but by Him. He not only
reveals God, but in contact with Him we *see* God,
we contact Reality, the Ultimate. We see through
Him into the world of God, and through Him the
world of God speaks to us. So utterly different is
His love for all men, so unbelievably fresh His
words among all those the sages have spoken, so
incomprehensibly new His deeds to all other good
deeds, so beyond human description and category, so
complete and adequate, are His person, His death,
His ways! He is Emmanuel. God is with men.

Christianity's message is Jesus Christ! He is not
merely a historic Person but an *a priori* origin, a
present living Christ, the promise of a future victory.
It is the task of the world to enter into Him to have
life. Tell the Good News! This message is the
central objective, the unitive element, that binds
together the various theologies of the New Testament. It is the redemption of the historical method
which divided the faith of the New Testament into
its several viewpoints.

Certainly, there are different gates whereby one
may enter into the Kingdom, but they are united in
this *naïve* gospel of God. Some may enter by way
of the Synoptics, others by the portals of John, still
others by the gate of Paul and the Hebrews. Protestantism certainly has affinities with all three, although its genius was chiefly in the Pauline type.
Even then, there is a dualism in John which ascribes

salvation alone to God's initiative. The gospel is not
a religious construction of men, but an assurance, a
faith, a hope, a salvation which is God's gift to a
helpless and lost humanity. T. R. Glover has repeatedly remarked about the variety of viewpoints of
Christians in the New Testament, as Streeter has
remarked about the variety of organizational polities
to be found in the New Testament. But today a new
emphasis is needed upon the unity of the essential
message and order that holds them all so warmly
together.

This message is past, present, and future. It is
both individual and social. There is but one gospel.
And it centers in love, the marvelous love of God
that stoops to share, even as it judges all men; and
the call to men to love Him and the neighbor in
turn, since they all belong together, *because of God*,
not because of man.

It is God who gives men life. God's person is
the sole Christian justification for our concern for
the freedom of all men. It is God's love and
righteousness that reveals man's sinfulness and prodigality. It is God's kingdom that makes us labor for
its coming. It is God's mercy that constantly sus-
tains us in this sinful world of which we are an
organic part, even though we may be called to be
saints. It is God who sets our bounds and it is God
who saves. God's will is our peace, and God's rod
and staff comfort us. It is God who gives us the
power to affirm life in bad circumstances. It is God
who lifts up our heads, and it is God who hallows our

human relationships.   It is God and only God who will give health to our social life.   God alone can be the only *safe* authority for any life, for only as we live in the authority of His truth and life and love have we any being and freedom.   God gives the glory and the crown to human existence, and because of Him *alone* do we know that there will be a future.

God, and God and Father of Jesus Christ alone, is The Only Reason!   He is not the God we make, but the God who is God, who reveals *Himself*.   This is the Christian message.   It must be told to the world by men who do not argue whether it is true or not, but who proclaim it out of a believing and simple heart!

This Book